ALSO BY JEFFREY MADRICK

Taking America

THE END
OF AFFLUENCE

Jeffrey Madrick

THE END
OF AFFLUENCE

The Causes and Consequences

of America's Economic

Dilemma

RANDOM HOUSE

NEW YORK

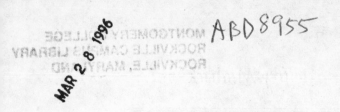

Copyright © 1995 by Jeffrey Madrick

All rights reserved under International and
Pan-American Copyright Conventions. Published in the
United States by Random House, Inc., New York,
and simultaneously in Canada by
Random House of Canada Limited,
Toronto.

Library of Congress Cataloging-in-Publication Data
Madrick, Jeffrey G.
The end of affluence : the causes and consequences of America's
economic decline / Jeffrey Madrick
p.   cm.
Includes bibliographical references and index.
ISBN 0-679-43623-5
1. United States—Economic conditions—1971–1981.   2. United States—
Economic conditions—1981–   I. Title.
HC106.7.M27   1995   330.973'092—dc20
95-19946

Manufactured in the United States of America
on acid-free paper
24689753
First Edition

For Matina, Michael,
and Christopher

ACKNOWLEDGMENTS

I have involved many people in the writing of this book. Some I gave no choice. My brother, Rob, took time from a tedious schedule to read drafts and make consistently invaluable suggestions. My daughter, Matina, provided a constant sounding board for new ideas. My parents and sister were sources of support, as were several friends who read drafts of this book, made contributions to my thinking, and invariably cheered me up at critical moments. They include Carol Jenkins, Donald Sutherland, Eddie Lawrence, and Lynne Francy. I am grateful to several economists and historians, including Sean Wilentz, Benjamin Friedman, Richard Nelson, Margaret Blair, and William Wolman, who read a draft of this book and made suggestions or corrections, many of which were eagerly taken.

Among the hundreds of scholarly sources I relied on, I would especially like to acknowledge the work of Alfred Chandler, Gavin Wright and Richard Nelson, and Michael Piore and Charles Sabel. This book disagrees with all of them in important ways, as they do with one another. But their pioneering insights were a platform without which I could not have gone my own way. Other economists and historians whose work was especially important for this book were Richard Freeman, Robert Margo, Claudia Goldin, Herbert Stein, Bennett Harrison, Gordon Wood, Charles Sellers, Angus Maddison, Frank Levy, Richard Murnane, Lawrence Mishel, Nathan Rosenberg, Paul Romer, and Edward Wolff. In general, the work of economic historians has gone unsung by the popular media. In doing my research, I have come to admire them, and I suspect as we continue to search for answers to our current plight, we will increasingly call on them for help.

Last, but in fact first, my editor, Jason Epstein. Countless writers will confirm that working with Jason is a collaboration. Everyone in the business knows that he forces you with an iron hand to write as clearly and succinctly as you are able. But he also enables you to think as boldly as you can. For that I am particularly grateful. Many thanks as well to his inspiring assistant, Joy de Menil.

CONTENTS

THE END
OF AFFLUENCE

Chapter 1

Two Decades of
Slow Growth

Like the clock that loses a second an hour, the American economy has lost ground so gradually over the past twenty years that we don't realize how far behind we have fallen. The economic expansion of the first half of the 1990s has made it even more difficult for Americans to judge how weak our economy has been over the past two decades compared with the rest of our industrial history. The main reasons for this decline are not inflation, government budget deficits, low levels of investment, faltering education, the irresponsibility of Democrats or Republicans, excessive spending on the military, the aged, or the poor—or the many other explanations for America's economic dilemma that we repeatedly hear. Rather, these presumed causes are themselves largely the consequences of a more persistent problem: a sharp slowdown in economic growth from our historical average of about 3.4 percent a year, and often higher, since the Civil War to a little more than 2 percent a year since 1973.[1] Meanwhile, our economic expectations have not declined accordingly. For the most part, we and our government carry on as though our economy were still growing at its historical rate. The results are repeated disappointment in our personal lives, waning confidence in long-standing institutions, and rising cynicism in our public life that threaten our best convictions as a nation.

To most of us, the apparently small decline in the annual rate of growth may not seem like much. We are, after all, a vast and rich economy, and we are still growing, even if more slowly. But the impact of slow growth, like the compound interest in a savings account, accumulates rapidly over time, and eventually makes a huge difference. During the mid-1970s, the loss of a percent a year in the rate of growth was on average a relatively small $100 billion a year. By 1993, however, the damage had grown enormously. In that year alone the gap between what the U.S. economy might have produced had we grown since 1973 at about our historical rate and what we actually did produce amounted to $1.2 trillion after inflation. This translates into approximately $4,600 of lost production for every American man, woman, and child. Over the twenty years since 1973 the accumulated losses in goods and services due to slow growth have come to nearly $12 trillion, or more than $40,000 a person.[2]

The stylized graph on the facing page shows how quickly

the losses caused by reduced growth accumulate. Between 1870 and 1973, and despite the many ups and downs in good times and bad, the U.S. economy had grown, as noted, at an average rate of 3.4 percent a year, excluding the effects of inflation. But between 1973 and 1993 (the last year for which we have complete data) the average rate of growth flattened to 2.3 percent a year after inflation, even though the workforce was expanding rapidly. In the graph below, the cyclical ups and downs of the economy are smoothed into straight lines. The graph represents how the rate of growth of gross domestic product (GDP) has declined from its historic norm and how

THE WEDGE WIDENS
Lost Production Due to Slow Growth

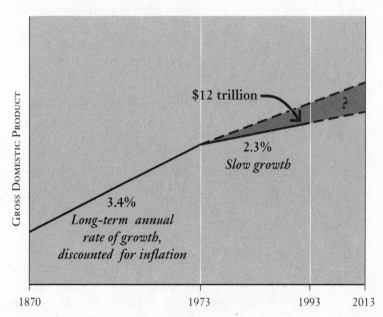

the gap between the norm and the actual performance of the economy since 1973 widens. The shaded area in between shows how an initially small loss in income and production expands over twenty years.

The enormity of the $12 trillion shortfall since 1973 can be envisioned in many ways. Twelve trillion dollars is more than enough to have bought each of America's homeowners a new house, or paid off all of our government, mortgage, and credit-card debt, or replaced all of our nation's factories, including capital equipment, with new ones.[3] As the shaded portion grows over time, so does the cumulative damage, so that by the year 2013, the total shortfall, assuming the economy grows at about 1 percent a year less than our historical norm, will amount to more than $35 trillion of lost production since 1973. If the population grows from 260 million to 310 million as expected, this will amount to a loss of well over one hundred thousand dollars a person.

This graph, then, is the economic expression of why we feel the way we do today. In the shaded area lie our lost jobs, falling and stagnating wages, eroding markets, closed factories, rising level of poverty, insecure pensions, and reduced homeownership. Though we blame it on other things, the widening gap between what had been our normal rate of growth for a century and the actual performance of the economy is the main source of the American public's declining confidence, which has shown up in survey after survey since the early 1970s. It explains why, by the 1992 presidential election, most Americans believed the nation had turned down the wrong economic road, and why, by the elections of 1994, despite several years of a moderate economic expansion, they still felt the same way.

Another useful, if more technical, way of looking at the extent of our decline since 1973 is to see how sharply the rate of growth itself has fallen from its historical level. It is illustrated in Figure 1 in the Appendix, which shows that the rate of growth has dropped by almost a full third. To raise growth back to its former rate of more than 3 percent a year, the economy would have to grow over time almost half again as fast as it has actually grown since 1973. In round terms, as economist Herbert Stein says, "The difference between 2 percent and 3 percent growth is not 1 percent, it is 50 percent."[4]

Though economic growth remained subnormal on average between 1973 and 1993, there were periods when prosperity seemed to return. In fact, we were told that our economic problems were solved whenever the rate of growth temporarily quickened. As we can see in Figure 2 in the Appendix, in both the 1970s and 1980s there were stretches of several years in which the economy expanded at an average rate of nearly 5 percent a year. Yet the average rate of growth since 1973, as represented by the dark line, never rose higher than 2.5 percent a year. These spurts of growth were neither strong enough nor sustained enough to compensate sufficiently for the steep recessions that preceded them or the unusually slow growth over the remaining years of the two-decade period.

Despite the economic expansion of the 1990s, and the claims by some economists that the economy was now growing too fast, economic growth as of late 1994 was again not robust enough to raise the long-term rate more than marginally. As of the end of 1994 the rate of growth since the end of the moderate recession in the spring of 1991 averaged only about 3.5 percent a year (compared with nearly 5 percent a year at this stage in several previous expansions). As we know, the rate of growth over the twenty years that ended in 1993 was only 2.3 percent a year. The annual rate of growth reached 4 percent during 1994, but even so, the long-term rate of growth since 1973 would rise to only 2.4 percent a year.[5]

On the other hand, any serious slowdown or recession in coming years would again reduce this long-run average performance significantly. Such a slowdown became increasingly likely when the Federal Reserve raised interest rates several times in 1994. The Federal Reserve reasoned that given the slow growth of our productive capacity over the preceding decades the economy could not grow as quickly as it once did without risking substantially higher inflation. Too much demand would be chasing too little capacity. Although the Federal Reserve may have raised rates prematurely, as some critics maintain, financial markets might well have pushed interest rates to restrictive levels even if the central bank had not acted.[6] For these and other reasons, which we will discuss later, a significant slowdown or even a recession was likely by 1995 or 1996, keeping our long-term economic performance far below our historical rate of growth.

How does such a slowdown in the rate of growth affect

most of us? Let's look first at the impact on the federal deficit. Had the economy grown about 1 percent a year faster, federal tax revenues would have been roughly $2.4 trillion greater over twenty years than they actually were, assuming existing rates of taxation. Had all this income been retained by the government, the national debt of $4 trillion could have been cut by well over half. Alternatively, the government could have reduced taxes by some proportion of this additional revenue. Had the government committed this sum to debt reduction, however, it would probably have saved more than $1.2 trillion in interest payments over these years. In most years since 1973, the federal government would have run only a small annual deficit at worst had growth remained closer to its historical average, so that by the late 1980s there would have been no federal deficit at all. By fiscal year 1993 there would have been a substantial surplus in the budget. Federal tax revenues in 1993 would have been about $300 billion higher and interest expense much lower, even if interest rates remained as high as they were, not only eliminating altogether the 1993 federal deficit of about a quarter of a trillion dollars but creating a substantial surplus as well. In other words, had we grown about 1 percent a year faster since 1973 than we did, which would still have left us slightly below our historical rate of 3.4 percent a year, all other things being equal we could have easily afforded the rising cost of government and reduced taxes as well.

Now, let's consider the impact on jobs and incomes. A rea-

sonable approximation is that slow growth since 1973 resulted
in the loss of several million jobs, mostly among the already
poor, less educated, and first-time job seekers, whose unemployment added billions to the cost of government. More significant for the economy as a whole, faster growth would have
increased demand for, and the value of, labor in general, so
that wages and salaries on average would have been higher.
For the typical family, annual income would probably have
been about $5,500 a year higher in 1993, and possibly more.
Over twenty years, the typical family would conservatively
have earned an additional $50,000 in total, assuming the same
employment pattern as prevailed in the 1980s. The extra income would, among other things, have allowed many more
young couples to buy a first home, many poor workers to buy
health insurance, and the typical middle-class family to pay
for housing and buy more of the goods and services it needed
without requiring a spouse to go to work or the main bread-
winner to take on a second job.

Let's also look at the level of investment in capital equipment, education, and physical infrastructure, one of our
biggest concerns over these years. The money for such investment comes from business profits, individual savings, and the
budgets of state and local governments. Had we grown at
about our historic rate, a reasonable estimate of the additional
capital available for investment from higher individual savings and corporate profits would have been about $700 billion
over twenty years, without any increase in our savings rate or

profit margins. State and local governments, which over these years have reduced services, failed to repair their roads and mass-transportation systems, and often cut spending on education, would have collected an additional $900 billion in income and corporate taxes. Local economies of course grow at various rates. But to take one example, had the economy of the state of Iowa grown by 1 percent more a year since 1973, it would have had approximately $3 billion more in tax revenues. Instead, it raised sales taxes twice, had to plug an annual budget deficit that had grown to nearly $500 million by 1993, and put a spending cap on social programs.

Our health-care expenditures, our fastest-growing major expense, would have been more affordable if we had continued to grow at the historic rate. About 14 percent of everything we spend now goes for health care, compared with 9 percent or 10 percent in other advanced nations. But had our economy grown at its historic rate, the same level of health expenditures would have been a more comfortable 11 percent to 12 percent. Similarly, presuming we borrowed no more, the burden of household and corporate debt that we took on would have been more manageable. With a far lower national debt, the federal government in turn might have been able to borrow enough money prudently to reform welfare and provide such social goods as day care and health insurance to the millions who couldn't afford it. It would also have been able to stimulate the economy more readily in times of recession by raising its level of spending. Because of the high level of debt, the use of such countercyclical policies to minimize the duration of recessions is now limited.[7]

=

To most of us, it may still defy common sense that so small a decline in the rate of growth can have such consequences. We generally presume, and are often told by the experts, that we have lived through worse times before. Some insist that in the last twenty years we have merely given back some of the unusual gains made in the twenty-five years after World War II when we easily dominated world markets and American workers enjoyed rapid gains in income.

But by the early 1990s the record of the prior two decades was clearly unusual by any standard in American history. Measures of our early economic growth as a nation are not as reliable as current data are, but they show that over no other peaceful twenty-year period since the Civil War, and possibly since the early 1800s, excepting the years that included the Great Depression, did the economy grow as consistently slowly as it has in the past twenty years. In fact, the economy grew as fast as it did only because baby boomers born after World War II entered the workforce in huge numbers, the number of workers expanding one and a half to two times faster than the total population. Had the economy been as robust as it was in the past, GDP per capita should have grown much faster in the 1970s and 1980s than its long-term average because a much higher proportion of the population was now working. But GDP per capita grew at only 1.3 percent a year, a full percent slower than it did between 1948 and 1973, and half a percent slower than its average growth rate of 1.8 percent a year since 1870.[8] Had GDP per capita grown at only 1.8 percent a year since 1973, the combined increase in federal tax revenues and reduced interest payments would still have wiped out the entire federal deficit by 1993.

What is more, the rate of growth between 1948 and 1973 of nearly 4 percent a year, which some now maintain was unsustainably fast, was not unique in America's industrial history. As we have seen, we had been growing at 3.4 percent a year since 1870 after inflation. But if we go back to 1820, when our economy was first beginning to grow rapidly, the average rate of growth from this smaller base has been 3.7 percent a year after inflation. Between 1870 and 1910, when our industrialization was fully under way and the economy was already quite large, the rate of growth averaged 4 percent a year, and rapid growth persisted far longer than did the similarly rapid rate of growth after World War II.[9] It was not the first two post–World War II decades, then, that were especially unusual compared with our historical record, it was the two decades of slow growth that began in 1973.

=

The foundation of economic growth is productivity, whose rate of growth has declined even more steeply than our overall economic growth since 1973. Growing productivity—the economy's output of goods and services per hour of work—is the reason the average person's standard of living rises. Conversely, without growing productivity, incomes typically stagnate. An economy would then grow only as fast as its working population grew.

Since a few years after the Civil War, productivity has grown at an average rate of about 2 percent a year (even including the Great Depression). In other words, workers produced an average of 2 percent more each year for every hour they worked. Beginning in the 1890s, the rate of productivity growth picked up to about 2.3 percent. At that point America had become the most productive country in the world, producing more per hour of work than any other country, and it retained its huge lead over most countries until well after World War II. In the immediate post–World War II period, the rate of productivity growth rose to 2.7 percent a year.[10]

But since 1973 the average annual growth of productivity has fallen to .9 percent a year—so far as we can tell, the worst twenty-year showing since the end of the Civil War (again excepting the first few years of the Great Depression).[11] The widely heralded Reagan economic expansion did nothing to correct this fundamental problem. The growth of productivity remained about as slow during Reagan's two administrations as it had become in Ford's and Carter's. In fact, as we have seen, we would have grown even more slowly in the 1970s and 1980s had the workforce not expanded so rapidly. This performance stands in contrast to our past record when we both raised productivity and absorbed millions of new workers at the same time. For example, between 1870 and 1910, when the working-age population grew even more rapidly than it had in the 1970s and 1980s, our economy still produced gains in productivity of 2 percent a year.

Once adjusted for the ups and downs of the business cycle, productivity so far in the 1990s is again growing no faster than it did in the 1970s and 1980s. In fact, overall productivity has been growing at almost the identical rate over the course of the economic expansion since 1991 as it did over the expansive phases of the business cycle in the slow-growing seventies and eighties. Economic data are always subject to interpretation, of course, but claims that productivity is climbing strongly in the 1990s typically ignore or underestimate the cyclical nature of its growth. Moreover, revisions in the data are likely to reduce the productivity growth reported so far in the 1990s even further (see Chapter 6). "The real mystery of the post-1973 slowdown is the sharp deceleration of productivity growth in the . . . USA," writes the British economist Angus Maddison.[12] To this mystery we shall soon return (see Figure 3 in the Appendix).

Also unprecedented over so long a period was the fall in average wages. Whatever changes had occurred in the economy in these two decades had clearly hit the American worker hardest. Slow-growing productivity inevitably dampens gains in salaries and wages because we don't produce as much in goods and services per worker, and therefore we don't produce as much income per worker, either. But most American workers since 1973 fared significantly worse than even slow productivity growth warranted. The highest proportion of new jobs over these years was created in low-paying service industries, where productivity gains were hard to attain, while many higher-paying manufacturing and related jobs were eliminated or filled by temporary or lower-wage workers, often in companies abroad or in low-wage regions of the United States.[13] Workers no longer got nearly the wage increases over time that they had expected as they stayed on the job or rose through the ranks. Workers in each age group typically made less than those who came before them. A growing proportion of workers lost ground, incomes falling below the levels they attained when they were younger and less experienced. Overall, discounted for inflation, the average weekly wages of so-called non-supervisory workers, about 80 percent of the workforce, fell by 15 percent from 1973 to 1993 (see Figure 4). Even if we include the growth of pension, health, and other worker benefits over these years, the compensation of a typical worker today has fallen compared with what it was for the typical worker twenty years ago, after discounting for inflation, and it has fallen sharply on average for young, high school–educated, and minority workers.[14]

By about 1987 slow economic growth had begun to put pressure on the salaries of better-paid white-collar workers as well. These wages fell in that year, and did so continually throughout the economic recovery that began in 1991. As a result of these factors, the average real income of families was only a few percentage points higher in 1993 than in 1973, and that largely because so many more spouses were working.[15] There have been shorter periods when wages have fallen sharply, but as far as we can tell, there has been no other twenty-year period since 1820 when average real wages fell, with the possible exception of the years just before and after the Civil War.[16]

One result of these gradual, almost unnoticed changes was, of course, that as our incomes stopped growing, we saved less and borrowed more in the 1980s to maintain our standard of living. Meanwhile, as tax revenues grew more slowly, government also borrowed more to meet its own obligations. Having borrowed so much, we found ourselves without the expected amounts of money to invest in upgrading our public infrastructure and education. Moreover, with incomes stagnating for so long, we were less willing than ever to pay higher taxes. Thus, when President Clinton insisted early in his administration on the need to reduce our borrowing by spending less and taxing more while putting a little aside to invest in such areas as job training, business development in cities, and a youth service program, the public resisted anything more than modest changes. Even a $3 billion package of aid to victims of the 1993 summer flood in the Midwest met resistance. Five billion dollars for job retraining was hard to find. Small tax-hike proposals were fought tooth and nail. By 1994 even the popular crime bill was hard to pass mainly for lack of money, whereas in the past large tax increases were paid by the public from a significantly rising standard of living or to pay for a major war. In early 1995 Congress refused to pass a $40 billion loan guarantee for Mexico to stay a financial crisis there, a guarantee that probably would never have been called upon.

If we don't make up for our lost growth since 1973, and overall we continue to grow only between 2 percent and 2.5 percent a year for another twenty years rather than at our historical norm, the compounding effects will take a far bigger toll. In addition, we will no longer have the benefit of a rapidly growing workforce. Between 1993 and 2013, roughly another $24 trillion, or more than $75,000 a person in today's dollars, could be lost in addition to what has already been lost in the past twenty years because of a reduction of 1 percent a year in our rate of growth. In total, it would be as if everyone in America were to stop working for two or three years. The reduced tax revenue to the federal government would amount to more than $4 trillion over the next twenty years, or about two and a half years' worth of current government expenditures. In the year 2013 alone, the typical family could earn $11,000 less, about one third of what it earns annually today.[17] Many economists believe we will not grow by more than 2.5 percent a year for the foreseeable future. Yet numbers like these change history.

=

Many factors help explain this decline in America's growth. The list is familiar. Success bred complacency. Old ways of doing business became encrusted and corporate bureaucracies discouraged change. Political and policy errors took their toll, from overexpanding the economy in the inflationary 1970s to taking on debt in the 1980s, which drove interest rates and therefore the dollar to debilitating heights. So did the costs of the Cold War, including the Vietnam war. American consumers saved too little and spent too much. Foreign nations, having had to rebuild from scratch after World War II, had more modern capital equipment than we did.

But the extent and abruptness of the slowdown since 1973 demand further explanation. Twenty years of slow growth is a long time—long enough to produce significant social and political consequences, and long enough so that we must now take seriously the possibility that we may be suffering not from a series of recessions from which we will eventually recover but from a substantial change in our fortunes that will not correct itself or respond to government policies. No one can say with confidence whether or not a new prosperous chapter in America's history will open soon, but it is possible that our slower economic growth is no longer simply cyclical or temporary but structural and permanent. We are not prepared for this. Americans are the only people in the world who take fast growth for granted as a natural consequence of their country's uniquely prosperous history. Our instinctive response to our problems, our sense of what is right and good, the means by which we earn our self-respect, and our view of our role in the world have been formed by a history of unusual economic advantage. Unlike most of our advanced rivals, we have had little experience with inherent limits to expansion.

It cannot be said strongly enough that the economy we

have come to take for granted has been remarkable. By the 1880s, the size of the U.S. economy had surpassed Britain's, whose lead was thought insurmountable. We were more productive than Britain—we produced more goods and services per hour of work—by sometime in the 1890s.[18] A comparison with Germany's nineteenth-century economy is especially instructive. Germany's powerful industrial revolution did not get fully started until 1870. By that time America's industrial revolution had been well under way. Starting from a much lower base, therefore, Germany's rate of growth would have been expected to exceed America's, at least for a while. Yet despite Germany's takeoff (the fastest of a major European nation over these years), the American economy continued to grow faster. In 1870 America's per capita GDP was $2,247. In terms of dollars, Germany's was only $1,300. By 1913 America's GDP per person more than doubled to $4,850 while Germany's didn't quite double to $2,606. All this time, America was providing jobs for tens of millions of immigrants.[19]

America's fast growth continued until the early 1970s, though the rate of growth was tested time and again by severe recessions and financial collapses. There were nine significant recessions between 1870 and 1913, three of which were especially severe. The depression of the 1870s, for example, was almost as lengthy as the Great Depression of the 1930s. In the 1890s production fell by more than 15 percent and the unemployment rate remained above 15 percent for four years. The recession of the early 1900s was almost as steep. But after each setback, the economy recovered and resumed its fast pace of growth. Because both productivity and the population were growing strongly over this period, the average rate of annual growth remained around 4 percent a year.[20]

During the early years of the Great Depression, production fell by more than 30 percent. The economy crawled back only to plunge again in the second half of the decade. But so powerful was the underlying strength of the economy that the lost production was entirely made up soon after our entrance into World War II. After the war, recessions were milder. Production rarely dropped by more than a few percent partly because of government guarantees, including so-called automatic stabilizers, such as unemployment insurance, and financial safeguards, such as insurance on bank deposits, as well as management of the economy through fiscal and monetary stimulus. Only after 1973 did the economy expand less vigorously than it had in the past, while recessions themselves had steepened compared with the early post–World War II period.[21]

According to the calculations of Angus Maddison, who has compiled the historical growth rates of the world's leading nations, the American economy grew on average by 3.7 percent a year between 1820 and 1989, as we have noted, over which time America's GDP rose by 450 times. No other country came close. Germany grew by 2.5 percent a year, its GDP rising by only sixty times over the same period, and Japan grew by 2.8 percent a year, its GDP rising by about one hundred times. Britain was the notable laggard. While its lead was enormous in 1820, it grew at only 2 percent a year on average since then, so that by 1989 Britain's GDP had risen by only twenty-seven times since 1820. Such is the damage done by consistently slow growth. Since the early 1800s, America's population grew by more than 2 percent a year while the populations of the other nations grew far more slowly. Yet even measured in terms of growth per capita, the American economy outpaced that of every other major nation until after World War II.

=

Where do we now stand in our economic history? The answer to this question will occupy the next few chapters. But we should begin by examining just what sustained America's unusual rate of growth over so long a period and what actually happened to change it. The most influential nineteenth-century interpretation of America's economic expansion was made by Frederick Jackson Turner in 1893. The young historian was trying to make sense of disturbing changes in the American economy as the agrarian economy gave way to an industrial one—changes that confused us then as much as current changes do today.

Turner argued that the American experience was formed largely by our vast and open frontier, where the ratio of people to land, so high in Europe, was for us uniquely low. This economic advantage had provided ample opportunity for Americans to acquire fertile, cheap, often free land, enabling the majority to become economically independent. But when the Census of 1890 reported that the frontier had been at last filled up, Turner believed America's distinctive advantage had been lost. "Never again will such free gifts of land offer themselves," he said. "The frontier is gone and with its going has closed the first period of American history."[23] He worried that after nearly a century of economic opportunity America might have reached a turning point, and believed that we would have to look outside our boundaries to find sources of new growth. Turner's gloomy thesis was consistent with the imperial longings that gripped many Americans at the turn of the century.

Turner was wrong, of course. Even as he wrote, industrialization was providing a second, even more potent frontier of renewed economic opportunity to new generations of Americans. But despite his oversimplifications, Turner articulated something essential about what held us together as a nation. His was the first broad economic interpretation of America's history. He understood that unusual, even abnormal economic opportunity had been the one long unbroken strand in American experience, which had created America's distinctive characteristics, including its optimism. "Since the days when the fleet of Columbus sailed into the waters of the New World, America had been another name for opportunity," Turner said. "So long as free land exists, the opportunity for a competency exists."[24] What Turner could not imagine was that there would be any other basis for this opportunity than access to land, and he was deeply concerned about what would happen to us without it.

If Turner underestimated the benefits of commerce and industrialization, he was right about the powerful appeal of the frontier in our early years. From the beginning, cheap, fertile land provided unusual economic opportunity and attracted migrants in remarkable numbers. Western New York filled rapidly after the Revolution, the state's population quadrupling in only two decades. Between 1780 and 1800 the population of Tennessee grew by ten times. Only a generation after it was settled in 1820 Ohio had a population of five hundred thousand people, making it the fifth-largest state in the union. The acquisition of new territory kept pace. The Louisiana Purchase of 1803 alone doubled America's territory.[25] Eventually, the United States would nearly double in size again. Acquiring new territory was one of the most important of presidential priorities in our first half century or so. Thomas Jefferson assured the public in his first inaugural address that land would be available "to the hundredth and thousandth generation."[26]

Even later in the century, during the first stages of industrialization, the search for economic opportunity at the frontier remained a way of life for many. The population of Boston, for example, grew by only 387,000 people between 1830 and 1890, yet well over 3 million people had lived there at one time or another over these years before moving west.[27] "We are a rapidly—I was about to say fearfully—growing country," said John Calhoun early in the century, when the U.S. population was young, vigorous, and expanding by nearly 40 percent a decade. As late as 1820 only 5 percent of Americans lived in cities, compared with nearly one third of England's population.[28]

On the farms early Americans lived with what would be considered today a bare minimum of necessities. "A majority of free Americans lived in a distinctive subsistence culture remote from river navigation and the market world," writes historian Charles Sellers.[29] But compared with Europe, the average standard of living in colonial America was enviable. In England, three fourths of the land was owned by the gentry, but most of those who worked the land in America owned their piece of it. Throughout the new nation, poverty was not onerous and famine not a serious concern as it was throughout Europe.[30] This is the "best poor man's country in the world," said one colonial observer, provided of course that you were white.[31] Economic historians have concluded that the average standard of living in the United States was rising only modestly in the colonial and immediate post-Revolutionary years. But access to land was so ample that it allowed the overwhelming number of new Americans to acquire a minimal standard of living and a significant degree of economic independence.[32]

America's optimistic, individualistic, and self-reliant ideology was emboldened by the economic success on the frontier. "These free lands promoted individualism, economic equality, the freedom to rise, democracy," wrote Turner.[33] What was clear was that in the early years, when these "distinctly American" characteristics, to use Turner's description, were applied to the task of eking out a living, they seemed to work.

One result was that Americans developed a special intolerance for poverty. Though there were almshouses before the Revolution, when the common wisdom ascribed poverty to divine will, by the nineteenth century poverty was regarded as a matter of individual responsibility. You could always go far enough west to find cheap land and feed yourself. Even when poverty increased later in the nineteenth century, Americans did not readily accept it. "This is a country of self-made men, and the idle, lazy, poor man gets little pity in his poverty," wrote the Reverend Calvin Colton.[34] As industrialization spread, many Americans refused to believe that hundreds of thousands of workers could be unemployed through no fault of their own. The Protestant ethic preached that hard work invariably led to material success and that material well-being was a sign of spiritual grace, a doctrine later expanded of course by social Darwinists who claimed that survival of the economically fittest was nothing less than a law of nature. Those who did not succeed might be pitied but should not be helped, a principle reemphasized by Herbert Hoover in the first years of the Great Depression. In a country where most citizens did better themselves, such an ideology easily took hold.[35] Mistrust of government and a stubborn sense of equality, Turner argued, had their roots in the frontier, where hard work, self-reliance, and optimism paid off.

Turner would cite Daniel Boone as the archetypal frontiersman who could maintain his independence by always moving farther west, keeping one step beyond civilization. It was a story that Americans not only relished but also adopted as part of their folklore. In the 1760s, Boone led his large family and a community of followers into Kentucky, where they cleared land, farmed for themselves, and hunted for game. Despite the well-known forays of Native Americans, Boonesborough, with only three hundred settlers, could support itself on what it hunted and what it farmed.[36] But after the Revolutionary War, Kentucky was the site of a land rush. From scarcely a soul when Boone got there, the population of Kentucky Territory grew to 20,000 people by the early 1780s. By 1800 there were more than 220,000 settlers in Kentucky.[37]

Boone was never clever enough to profit from the land rush, though recent research suggests that he tried to do so.[38] Disillusioned, he settled in Missouri Territory, on the other side of the Mississippi. There he and his family were again able to hunt and farm to support themselves. His complaints about the encroachment of civilization and government grew legendary, spread by the newspapers and idealized in a bestselling biography that was long on lore and soft on facts. His popularity tells us much about how we want to see ourselves. As his exploits were publicly romanticized, Boone seemed to isolate himself further. In his eighties, broke from speculating in land, he was still farming and hunting, and he remained our quintessential free, independent, self-reliant American man, a model for our literature and popular culture ever after.[39]

==

The economic age that depended on access to land ended long before Turner's lecture in 1893, however. Even when Boone died in 1820, a market economy, with a growing volume of trade dominated by rising towns and cities, had begun contributing to economic growth. By then, with the recent lifting of the embargo on trade with Britain, the American economy was on its way to dominate the world.[40]

Many farmers had become small businessmen themselves in these years, often selling their surplus crops both domestically and overseas. Agrarian exports were soaring, leading one observer to state that America was the "granary of Europe."[41] One study found that the distance wheat could be transported profitably doubled to one hundred miles in the forty years following the Revolution, so that by the early nineteenth century the wheat-export belt of America extended from Connecticut to Virginia and inland to the Shenandoah Valley. Cotton production, made especially competitive by cheap slave labor, had also moved farther inland.[42] The image of the simple farmer attached forever to his land is a romantically exaggerated one. Farmers widely speculated in land as the commercial boom sent prices up. They often settled on their farms for only a few years, sold out at a handsome profit, and moved farther west in the expectation of making another killing.[43]

By 1820 small-scale industrialization had also spread far more widely than was generally realized. A quarter of the working population of New England, for example, was employed in small textile and shoe factories by then. Many others worked at home. Adam Smith's specialization of labor was already raising productivity. Tasks were efficiently divided among those who made only shoe "uppers," for example, or others who sewed only the cuffs on garments. Farmers too took in textile work and had begun to manufacture some items, such as rudimentary iron tools. Even Jefferson, who once believed America would and should remain a nation of farmers, eventually admitted that manufactures were good for the country. Between 1790 and the beginning of Jefferson's trade embargo in 1807, American agricultural and manufacturing exports rose from about $20 million a year to more than $108 million. Tariffs were imposed on imports, and would mostly be kept high for the rest of the century in order to protect America's infant manufacturing industries.[44]

In these years the building of roads and canals became a national passion. Trade had risen by thirteen times on the Erie Canal between 1824 and the 1850s, and by twelve times on the Mississippi over the same period.[45] The first short railroad lines were put in during the 1830s and 1840s. Overall, despite several sharp depressions, the economy grew more quickly since the early 1800s than it ever had before, stimulated not solely by the swelling population but by something new in America: rising productivity. The best evidence is that between 1800 and 1850 the economy grew between 1 percent and 1.3 percent per person compared with less than .5 percent per person before that. Access to land still mattered, but less so; prosperity was now also being created by increasing agricultural and industrial productivity.[46]

By the 1850s the size of markets was growing dramatically. "Manifest destiny" was on everyone's lips and the nation's territory was expanded to the Pacific. Long rail lines were being laid for the first time that connected large cities in all the country's regions. Steamship lines grew rapidly as well. In all, goods that once took months to reach their destination now frequently got there in less than a week.[47] Domestic trade became a key to growth. The huge American market was an unparalleled free-trade zone, so to speak, where farmers and businesses could specialize in the production of what they did best. It was a diverse, thriving marketplace, where Adam Smith's assertions about the advantages of specialization and the division of labor could come to their fullest fruition.

=

The Civil War had interrupted the nation's growth. But once the nation was united again, the economy was spurred on by an industrial revolution whose strength no one could have anticipated. Manufacturing replaced trade as the focus of dozens of fast-growing cities. By 1900, 30 million Americans were in the workforce, some 10 million of whom worked in manufacturing. Millions more worked in the transportation, trade, and service businesses that supplied them. By then, nearly 40 percent of the population lived in the cities. Millions also worked in the increasingly valuable mines. This was America's second frontier.[48]

Modern research shows what Turner probably could not have known at the time of his lecture. In the 1880s, the nation manufactured as much in dollar volume of industrial goods as it had produced in wheat, corn, beef, poultry, and all other agricultural products. Even before Turner's lecture, the

United States produced more goods and services than Great Britain, and several times as much as the next largest economy, Germany. Driven by the spread of mass production, American products were now typically cheaper than those manufactured in other nations. As noted, total output per hour of work exceeded Britain's sometime in the late 1890s, making the United States the most productive large nation in the world.[49]

By the time of Turner's lecture the importance of the geographical frontier that he had so romanticized had long since begun to decline. By 1900 there were about 75 million people living in the United States, the large majority of them making a better living than they ever had before. As a result, America did not rebel, lose its direction, or renounce its basic ideology. To a large degree, though Americans were by no means as independent as they once were, now often working in highly regimented factories and living in dense cities, they believed that the characteristics that had propelled the economy in its earliest years continued to do so long after the industrial revolution had begun to make the first frontier less important. Economic opportunity still provided "competency" in America, and Americans still believed the true sources of their unique success were self-reliance, individualism, and hard work.

=

Industrialization brought with it a set of new problems. Unemployment became pronounced during industrial depressions. Over the century the distribution of income became more unequal, and the rising fortunes of the ostentatious robber barons in the 1880s and 1890s stood in sharp contrast to growing pockets of poverty and squalor in the cities. Work had been less hard on the farms than the often sixteen-hour workdays, six days a week in the cities. Labor strikes brought on by these conditions were thwarted by the courts or put down violently by employers, apparently without serious protest from the citizenry, even though many strikes did succeed in raising wages and improving conditions for their workers.[50]

However much the American ideology denied it, poverty now existed and it was palpable. In the slums of New York, Boston, and Chicago, workers often lived six in a room. A strong strain of pessimism crept into the American culture. Writers like Frank Norris and Upton Sinclair captured the rising discontent with a new moneyed culture. Respected intellectuals like Henry and Brooks Adams saw little hope for America's future. Populism, which flourished especially in southern and agricultural states, became a powerful political movement that demanded significant reforms and accused the big-city bankers of nailing Americans to a cross of gold.[51]

But time and again, rapid economic growth provided enough opportunity to appease most of America's rebels and doubters, even during politically turbulent times. Surging economic growth in the 1830s cemented Andrew Jackson's democratic reforms, just as it calmed populist discontent once the depression of the 1890s had ended. For all the political reforms, it was a rising real wage over time that was the great palliative. Despite "sweated" labor and occasionally severe depressions, real wages for most Americans rose rapidly between the 1870s and early 1900s. Overall, real wages, though they fluctuated widely, rose by about 1 percent a year on average over the entire century. The typical American was earning roughly three times as much after inflation in 1900 as in 1800.[52] Despite the arrival of so many millions of immigrants, the average American wage was still 50 percent higher at the start of World War I, measured in terms of purchasing power, than the average wage earned by a British worker.[53]

=

In the twentieth century, production and wages again rose dramatically. The second frontier turned out to have been only in its early stages. After a steep recession following World War I, the American economy again took off in the 1920s, up by 18 percent in 1922 alone. The use of electricity spread widely. The Model T had come to market a few years before the war and was a great success. Other new products included radios, gas ovens, and refrigerators, all selling at prices that made them affordable to a new mass market of American consumers. Productivity rose on average by 4 percent a year between 1922 and 1928.

The Great Depression was a major challenge to the new industrial economy, and to our political stability as well. Unemployment soared to about 25 percent of the labor force. It took the arms buildup before World War II, and ultimately the war itself, to get America back on its feet. While some prominent economists believed the economy could stagnate indefinitely, in fact the war merely demonstrated how powerful America's economic potential was. Production rose above its 1929 peak by 1940. Incomes rose to pre-Depression levels by 1942. Productivity was again on a fast track. Unemployment virtually disappeared.[54]

After World War II most analysts thought a return to recession, or even a severe depression, was all but inevitable. The sharp recession after World War I and the Great Depression were still fresh memories. But the second frontier proved far more durable than its critics supposed. After a brief recession the economy again expanded rapidly and the forecasts of long unemployment lines never materialized.

The fast growth after World War II was aided by the destruction of Europe and Japan during the war; the United States had the world market mostly to itself well into the 1950s. Returning veterans went to college in great numbers, financed by the GI Bill of Rights, and the emphasis on education spread throughout the nation. Wartime technological breakthroughs spilled over to profitable commercial uses. With government help, for example, Bell Labs developed the transistor in 1948. Timex produced a cheap watch based on government research. High military expenditures may also have promoted growth in the short run, though over time they eroded resources in a way that would dampen future growth.

The annual rate of economic growth of nearly 4 percent a year between 1947 and the early 1970s rivaled in pace, though not duration, the fast growth of the latter third of the nineteenth century. Family income after inflation doubled in this period. In the mid-sixties, the unemployment rate was only about 4 percent, yet inflation was inconsequential.

This second frontier was the answer to Turner's understandable concerns. For all its ups and downs, it produced the fastest, broadest-based economic growth and rising living standards a major economy had ever seen. There is not one forecast on record that suggested it might not last. One celebrated forecaster in the 1960s claimed that productivity would grow at a rate of 4 percent a year until the turn of the century.[55] America had no reason to doubt itself, or to challenge the validity of its original frontier ideology. Because of rapid economic growth, its confidence in itself had never been higher.

=

But the pace of growth was about to slow dramatically. There were several signs of this as early as the mid-1960s. Corporate profits as a percentage of sales began to decline rapidly, falling from about 14 percent of sales after taxes in 1965 to only 8 percent by 1970. The growth of productivity had also tapered off significantly to a rate of 2 percent a year from a rate of about 3 percent a year, even though capital investment was high.[56] Economists believed that at worst it was a temporary stall.

Only after the oil crisis in 1973, when the OPEC countries raised prices threefold, did we have the first serious recession of the post–World War II period. The economy did not begin to recover until mid-1975. Over the next seven years we experienced an inflationary spiral and the two other recessions we discussed earlier. The 1982 recession was even more severe than the OPEC-induced recession in 1974 and 1975. In sum, we suffered three recessions in the ten years between 1973 and 1982, two of which were the worst in the post–World War II period.

The Reagan expansion between 1983 and 1988 temporarily muted economic criticism. When the expansion petered out in 1989, however, the economy was only slightly ahead of its 1979 peak by most per capita measures, and most important, as we noted, the growth of productivity continued to lag badly for the second decade in a row. The Reagan expansion was followed by the four years of slow economic growth under President Bush, which included the recession in 1990 and part of 1991. The economic expansion that began in 1991 was only a moderate one, unable to reverse even modestly the damage done over the preceding twenty years. As of the fall of 1994 the average real wage had been falling for more than two decades, the rate of growth in productivity was still historically low, the poverty rate had risen significantly, and America could no longer invest adequately in its future without a significant sacrifice in current standards of living. Americans would say in survey after survey that they were beginning to feel that something had changed, but nevertheless they had continued to underestimate the impact that slow economic growth was having on their lives. This may have been only natural. Americans had never had to deal with an indefinite period of slow economic growth before, and most of us could not figure out exactly what had changed. Here our politicians, recalling how voters rejected Carter and Mondale for their candor about some of our economic problems, chose not to repeat their mistake. The media, which had learned the same lesson, were no better. Doom and gloom, to use the catchword of the times, did not sell. But President Reagan's optimism did.

Chapter 2

WHAT WE HAD

Carefully gathered data show that by the mid-1700s, the average income of American colonists measured in terms of purchasing power had already exceeded the average income earned in England.[1] Better diets even made Americans healthier than their Old World counterparts. Revolutionary soldiers, for example, stood three to four inches taller than their British adversaries. Our optimistic, confident sense of ourselves developed in these privileged circumstances, and, as we have seen, American income, though volatile, kept growing rapidly.[2]

Abundant land on the frontier, natural resources, a thriving domestic trade, and agricultural exports supported in part by slave labor accounted for this unusual prosperity in our early years.[3] But ingrained in most of us, I think, is the oversimplified idea that our exceptional growth since the Civil War has been almost entirely the consequence of the scientific, engineering, and technological breakthroughs of the nineteenth century, coupled perhaps with our enterprising attitude and a largely unregulated market economy. America had in fact no particular edge over other industrial nations in the development of the labor-replacing machines of the industrial revolution. The steam engine, the open-hearth furnace, and the internal-combustion engine, to name only a few, were invented in Europe. Similarly, the breakthroughs made by our own great inventors, from Eli Whitney to Thomas Edison, were known to European manufacturers.[4] Nor was capitalist initiative by any means an exclusively American quality. British investors roamed the world over, putting their money into risky new enterprises. German businessmen created a remarkable industrial boom after the Prussian victory in 1871 in the war against France. As for free markets, they had thrived everywhere from the Turkish bazaars to the shops of London long before the American economy took off.

What most distinguished America's post–Civil War industrial revolution was our enormous, continentwide marketplace, which enabled us to sell goods on a scale that could not nearly be matched by other countries. The mass production that resulted was not merely a matter of replacing labor with machines; all advanced countries accomplished this to one degree or other. Rather, American mass production was a highly complex system of production and distribution that reduced the costs of manufacturing each unit dramatically as the volume of production was raised. What made this increased production possible was a market large enough to absorb the goods that high-volume factories could produce. This only America had. Mass production also enabled us to exploit more fully our other major advantage, our abundant natural resources. The giant mass-production plants and equipment required large amounts of fuel and raw materials, which, in those years, only we could produce in such great quantities and therefore at such low cost.[5]

For nearly a century no other nation's mass-production industries were comparable to America's, nor was our rate of growth equaled by any other major country during this period.[6] Between 1870 and 1913, the eve of World War I, when our mass-production industries were being built, America's rate of growth rose, as we have noted, to nearly 4 percent a year. By contrast, Germany's GDP grew at only 2.8 percent a year from a much smaller base, Japan's at 2.3 percent, and France's at 1.5 percent. What is most extraordinary about the American performance is that even though our population grew far faster than Europe's over these years, our GDP per person also rose faster, growing at a rate of 1.8 percent a year between 1870 and 1913, while Germany's GDP per person grew at 1.6 percent, Japan's at 1.4 percent, France's at 1.3 percent, and Britain's at 1 percent a year.[7]

By 1913 we were by far the most productive major nation in the world. America was producing 25 percent more per worker than Britain, the world leader for more than a century, and about twice as much per worker as either Germany or

France. By World War I we were making more than 30 percent of the world's goods. Of the goods that we produced, the largest mass-production companies alone accounted for roughly one quarter and were the major customers for the goods and services of many smaller companies representing a large portion of the rest of the economy (see Figure 5 in the Appendix).[8]

Between the world wars, when the European economies had recovered from the destruction of World War I, there was good reason to believe that they would be able to catch up, at least to some significant degree, with American levels of productivity. Economists generally assumed that the best industrial technologies could be employed by any country that had what were considered the essential conditions for economic growth: advanced technology, finance, and a well-educated population. The major European nations had all these. But remarkably enough, evidence gathered by economic historians in recent years shows that no such convergence occurred. America generally retained its large lead in productivity over all other advanced nations, even though the Great Depression had damaged us more severely and longer than it had most of these other nations. The American advantage, then, was clearly still intact.[9]

Only after World War II did our advanced rivals begin to catch up to us. For the first time, they gained access to our huge marketplace on almost an equal basis with ourselves as tariffs and transportation costs came down. The leading nations of Europe also developed a more unified market among themselves. Only then were other nations able to take full advantage of mass production. And only then did their levels of productivity begin to converge rapidly with ours. In order to understand what we may have lost permanently, we must understand what we actually had during the time of our second frontier, the hundred years or so of exceptional economic growth that preceded our current slowdown.[10]

=

In the mid-nineteenth century Great Britain was a highly mechanized and urbanized nation, long the leader in the production of textiles, iron, and most of the other products associated with what is known as the first industrial revolution. It had been the most productive nation in the world since early in the century, adopting new labor-saving machines throughout its key industries. Its dominance coincided with the fact that the most prosperous consumer market at the time was the so-called golden quadrangle between London, Cardiff, Edinburgh, and Glasgow, where ultimately 10 million people lived. This market was densely populated and well connected by transportation. By the standards that were to come, English factories and the business organizations that served them were small and informal. But Britain, the unquestioned leader in technology and manufacturing in the mid-nineteenth century, foresaw no potential challengers.[11]

By the 1840s, however, America's markets, as we have seen, were growing rapidly. Canals and turnpikes had made transportation far more efficient, and domestic trade was thriving and had probably already become as important to the American economy as our agricultural and manufactured exports to Britain and Europe. But this American marketplace was to expand dramatically in the coming years with the development of the railroads. The first short rail lines in America were laid in the 1830s to connect nearby cities, waterways, and canals. By the 1840s, railroad technology had become efficient and largely standardized.[12] Still, in 1850, there were fewer than ten thousand miles of track laid and only one railroad line, the Erie Railroad, which ran from Worcester, Massachusetts, to Albany, New York, connecting two distinct regions.

During the 1850s, about twenty-one thousand miles of track were laid. Complete systems were built that connected the major cities along the Eastern Seaboard from north to south, and in turn these same eastern cities to the developing regions of the interior, including the Old Northwest around the Great Lakes. In 1830 freight took three weeks to go from New York to Chicago. By the late 1850s it took three days.[13] Railroads captured the entrepreneurial imagination of the time. The losers in the transportation battle were the canals and riverboat lines, only a generation after they had been developed. Railroads "provided a crushing blow to most inland water routes," wrote the railroad historian George Rogers Taylor, setting a pattern of continual industrial upheaval that characterized our economic progress ever since (though it is arguable that a network of waterways and canals would have served almost as well; see Chapter 4).[14]

In the 1830s a merchant in a small Michigan town received

his stock from New York City by arranging passage along the Erie Canal to Buffalo. Then he hired a vessel to carry his goods across Lake Erie to Detroit. From there horse-drawn wagons carried the goods the rest of the way. By the end of the 1850s, this was accomplished mostly overland by rail in a matter of days.[15]

After the Civil War the railroads expanded more rapidly. By the mid-1870s there was more than twice as much track laid in the United States as there had been in 1860, reaching coast to coast. Railroad companies were now easily the largest business concerns in the nation, importing both capital and labor from Europe, and creating enormous demand for capital goods, notably iron rails. The early influx of Irish and German immigrants did not produce enough new workers to satisfy the railroads' demand, and the companies sent representatives across Europe to encourage more workers to emigrate.[16]

The scale of change in the 1880s was enormous. In this decade alone, about seventy-five thousand miles of railroad track were laid, again doubling the amount of track in the country. The Pennsylvania already ran from New York to Washington and Boston, and west through Philadelphia, Chicago, and ultimately St. Louis. The Union Pacific tamed the West. The Santa Fe in the Southwest became the largest railroad in the world. The carrying capacity of the trains had also increased enormously, doubling between 1860 and 1890.[17]

The telegraph spread as rapidly. By the 1880s a merchant

could order goods instantaneously and receive them almost anywhere within about a week. Cities in the interior of the nation served by the railroads expanded at fabulous rates as trade boomed. These cities became sources of huge demand for goods and services, manufacturing centers themselves, and distribution points from which to supply the regions around them. By one estimate, only 13 percent of the American population was not reachable by rail or steamship by 1890.

The vast nation could now be crossed quickly and cheaply. In 1858 it cost nearly 37¢ a bushel to ship wheat by rail from Chicago to New York. By 1870 the cost had fallen to 26¢ a bushel. By 1890 it was 14¢ a bushel. Overall, the average rate per ton mile on the rails was about 2¢ just after the Civil War, already well down from its prewar level. By 1890 the rate had fallen to a penny, and transportation was much faster.[18]

Those who assume that rapid change—or, indeed, "future shock"—is novel to the post–World War II era should examine more closely the pace of change in these years.[19] America had built by far the largest commercial marketplace in the world, a huge tariff-free trade zone connected by low-cost transportation that made it as dense in economic terms as the comparatively tiny British Isles. In 1880, when Britain had about 16,000 miles of track, America had more than 90,000 miles, connecting an entire continent and one and a half times as many people. By World War I Britain had about 25,000 miles of track, while America had 240,000 miles, connecting a population of 92 million people, about twice as many as in Britain. America's income per person was about 30 percent greater than Britain's before World War I, so that the overall demand for goods and services in America was well over twice as large as Britain's. With a population 50 percent again as large as Germany's and a far higher income per person, Americans consumed three to four times as much in goods and services as the Germans did. From a colony of only about 2 million people, America had become an economic giant nearly 100 million strong.[20]

==

This unparalleled marketplace enabled American businessmen to take fullest advantage of the new mass-production technologies of the time, reducing costs to a fraction of what they had once been for a great variety of consumer and industrial goods. James Buchanan Duke, for example, was the first American to buy a machine invented in England that could perform almost all the separate tasks required to make a cigarette and far faster than workers could. The "continuous process" machine compressed the tobacco, wrapped it in paper, pasted it, rolled it, and cut it into the right lengths. Old-fashioned cigarette manufacturers could produce 3,000 cigarettes a day with manual labor. The Bonsack machine, named after its inventor, James Bonsack, required far fewer workers and would eventually make 120,000 cigarettes a day.

This was mass production. As a result of the reduced need for labor, and the sheer speed of processing goods, costs of production fell precipitously. The more you could sell, the lower would be your costs as higher volume was spread over a fixed amount of capital equipment and labor. At the time, a British manufacturer figured that the Bonsack machine cut the cost of the wages he paid from 48d. for every thousand cigarettes to a mere .3d., a reduction of 99 percent.[21]

With only a handful of these machines, James Duke was able to keep the price of a pack of cigarettes to a nickel and dominate America's cigarette business for decades. In the 1870s and 1880s all kinds of companies, such as the Diamond Match Company, Procter & Gamble, Campbell's Soup, Borden, and Heinz, adapted similar "continuous process" machines to their own needs. Entire factories were also organized along these principles, making the process of production as "continuous" as possible in order to increase the speed of "throughput." Even meat-packers increased their speed of production by using a moving hook hung from the ceiling on which a carcass was passed along from butcher to butcher. This forerunner of Henry Ford's assembly line was called a "disassembly" line. By the end of the 1880s, giant consumer-products and packaged-foods companies, aided in addition by the new refrigerated railroad cars, were selling their wares across the nation.[22]

Continuous processing and other mass-production innovations, including the expanding oil pipelines, quickly raised the average output of an oil still from two hundred barrels a day to one thousand. The cost of refining a barrel of kerosene fell from 6¢ to 3¢ in the late 1860s and to only 1.5¢ by the 1870s.[23] Before the Civil War a typical steel plant with several hundred workers produced only three thousand tons of steel a year. Toward the end of the century twelve men could roll three thousand tons of steel in a single day.[24] In 1880 steel rails cost $67.50 a ton to produce at a typical factory. By 1889 the cost fell to $29.95 a ton. Ten years later rails cost $17.63 a ton, a drop of about 75 percent, making America the world's low-cost producer.[25] Because steel was an important component of other manufactured goods, the low manufacturing cost gave the United States an additional advantage. As the new century got under way, America became a leading exporter of farm equipment, machinery, and engineering products. Alarmists in England talked about an American industrial invasion. Carnegie Steel itself produced more steel than Britain, France, and Germany combined. Many mechanical consumer products were mass-produced in these years, including firearms, clocks, sewing machines, wagons, and bicycles, as well as grains, flour, and a wide range of packaged and processed foods.

=

Service industries, which we typically think of as labor-intensive, also became far more productive over these years as a mass market grew for mass-produced goods. The railroads were a classic example of the rising productivity in service industries, carrying an increasing load of goods far faster than ever before.[26] America also built giant mass-distribution and retail companies, which for the most part could not be profitably replicated in such numbers in smaller markets overseas. Wholesalers, in fact, were among the first beneficiaries of mass production, taking full advantage of the cost savings that could be made by buying and selling in bulk. The term "economies of scale" usually refers to manufacturing plants: the more you manufacture in a given period of time, the lower the cost per unit of production. But the source of lower costs is exactly the same for these service industries. As the business historian Alfred Chandler writes, "They reduced the unit costs of distributing goods by making it possible for a single set of workers using a single set of facilities to handle a much greater number of transactions within a specific period than the same number of workers could if they had been scattered in many separate facilities." In 1880 two thirds of manufactured goods sold in America passed through the large wholesalers, which had quickly expanded from the East Coast to such frontier cities as St. Louis and Cincinnati.[27]

The large, growing cities also gave rise to many highly efficient department stores as well as to new retail and grocery chains. These took advantage of the cities' concentrated demand in order to turn inventory rapidly, and, like wholesalers, they were among the first beneficiaries of economies of scale, raising the productivity of their companies by enabling a smaller cadre of employees to handle a far greater volume of goods than they once could. Full-fledged department stores, including Macy's, Wanamaker's, and Jordan Marsh, began to appear in the 1860s. In these same years, giant wholesalers, such as A. T. Stewart and Marshall Field, expanded their small retail outlets into department stores as well. The Great

Atlantic & Pacific Tea Co. began to expand beyond lower Manhattan in the late 1860s. By 1880 it was operating one hundred stores in about a dozen states. Grand Union and others followed. Woolworth opened its first handful of stores in the 1880s.[28]

Because selling in ever-larger volume was the key to exploiting economies of scale, American manufacturers and distributors became aggressive marketers and advertisers to a degree still unmatched by companies overseas. Chandler has documented how the dominant manufacturers in various industries invariably invested heavily in distribution and marketing.[29] James Buchanan Duke spent as much as 25 percent of his cigarette revenues on advertising, for example. When he began to sell cigarettes, tobacco was still mostly chewed, not smoked, and he set about to change America's habits. So did scores of other American companies. The American breakfast-food industry was created out of whole cloth, for example, by millers trying to sell their excess production. Singer dominated the world market for sewing machines by aggressive, sophisticated marketing. Because mass production and distribution were so much less prevalent in Europe, firms there were generally less concerned than Americans with creating greater demand for their goods. As a consequence, they did not become as proficient at marketing.

Compared with firms in other countries, American corporations also evolved an efficient, command-style organizational structure, which was unmatched in its attention to detail and cost control. So-called scientific management reduced every task in the manufacturing process to its smallest components, with human effort itself as merely one component of a large machine. Work was divided and specialized into simple tasks, and then divided and specialized into even more simple ones. Rarely did any single worker perform all or even more than a few of the functions required to manufacture a product anymore. One worker would specialize in filing down a few parts of a gun to make them interchangeable. Another tightened a few bolts on a bicycle. The machine became not only a model but a metaphor for human organization (and, of course, in this age of reason, for the workings of nature itself), and the worker was essentially another cog in the process.[30]

Many of the first CEOs were army men, trained in engineering at West Point. They adapted the pyramidal structure of the armed forces to their new business organizations. Orders flowed from one CEO at the top to a second layer of vice presidents and ultimately to the workers, who were expected to obey without question. If this system was insensitive to a worker's individuality, or boredom, or the desire to manage his or her own work, it was well suited to managing an economy of giant, otherwise unwieldy companies. While American workers, many of them immigrants eager for opportunity, resisted demanding, unimaginative mass-production work, they did not do so nearly to the extent that European workers did when businessmen tried to impose mass-production principles on them.[31]

Finally, American businesses "learned by doing" to a de-

gree that companies in other countries, where mass production was put into practice far less widely, simply could not.
Study after study has shown that the countless small innovations made by trial and error on the factory floor were as important to American technological superiority as major
inventions and scientific breakthroughs, and often more so.
These small innovations included everything from reducing
leaks in refineries to fitting parts better, to changing the order
in which goods were assembled on the production line. No
matter how carefully they copied American business practices, those European companies that tried to adopt mass-
production techniques frequently found it difficult to run
their operations as efficiently as the experienced American
companies.[32]

=

Mass production, then, was greater than the sum of its
parts, compounding a series of advantages not only in
manufacturing but also in distribution, advertising, management, and ongoing technological innovation that could not
easily be duplicated elsewhere. Ultimately, no one managed
sheer size and high volume the way American business did.
Around the giant companies were thousands of satellite sup-
pliers that benefited from the efficiency and stability of the
giant firms they served. As they grew larger and honed their
own product lines to the needs of the increasingly standardized and fast-growing mass producers, these countless manufacturing and service satellites also grew more productive.

Theoretically, a single European plant could generate enough sales volume to produce at the same unit cost as an American one. In fact, several German, French, Swiss, and British companies became some of the biggest in the world. But the large number and interlocking nature of American mass-production and distribution companies, along with their satellites, created a qualitatively different environment from what prevailed overseas.[33] Meanwhile, American workers, with their newfound prosperity, were eager to buy up the new, affordable, mass-produced products, even though they were standardized and utilitarian at best. After all, they had little else to compare these products with. European consumers were accustomed to more individually crafted products, and resisted standardized fare. Had American consumers also resisted such products, our economy would have grown more slowly.[34]

The rapidly changing economic environment in the United States was harsh. In general, the giant mass-production and distribution companies required fewer and fewer workers per unit of output, raising fears that there would not be enough jobs for the expanding population, fears similar to those that prevail today. Because they were so much more productive, the large mass producers and distributors could undercut prevailing prices and put smaller, more specialized factories, retailers, and other companies out of business as well. As older products, ranging from candles to riverboats, became obsolete their manufacturers and related companies went out of business, often within a generation, costing countless American workers their jobs.

But in contrast to what is happening today, overall productivity grew so rapidly in these years that the higher incomes and economic growth that resulted created many more good jobs than were lost to more efficient technologies. In 1860 there were fewer than 1 million workers in the factories. In 1900, though manufacturers had become much more productive, they now employed 10 million American workers. A similar number worked in transportation, wholesale and retail trade, and mining, all these interconnected with expanding mass-production industries.[35]

On average, the rate of unemployment was probably slightly higher in the nineteenth century than it has been in the post–World War II period. But while workers lost their jobs more frequently, they were unemployed for shorter periods than they would be in later years.[36] Meanwhile the lower prices charged by mass manufacturers and distributors for almost all consumer products benefited working Americans, who as consumers had extra money to buy still more new products, prompting rapid economic growth and development of new industries. On average, consumer prices fell by 40 percent between 1870 and 1910 and prices for producer goods fell even further. It was as if the price reductions we see today in consumer electronics products, such as computers and stereo equipment, were to sweep across almost all consumer and producer industries.[37] The standard of living of most Americans rose rapidly over these years, and by the standards of the day, America remained easily the most inviting advanced nation on earth. Though poverty was rising, employees were often overworked in the factory, measures of health in cities declined, and reforms were justifiably in great demand, the sheer persistence of immigration is the best proof that America was still a land of opportunity compared with the rest of the world. Evidence shows that immigrants knew about the real economic conditions in America, yet they kept coming in great numbers.[38]

=

The greatest advances in mass production came early in the twentieth century. Henry Ford led the way. He progressed slowly, taking more than a decade to attain a goal most believed was unrealistically ambitious because an automobile with thousands of parts was far more difficult to mass-produce than steel or bicycles. But Ford was dogged, with a religious faith in mass production. He and his managers made many innovations along the way, culminating in the moving assembly line in 1913. The objective as always was to increase the speed of throughput, and, in that year, Ford had been able to reduce the time it took to manufacture a single Model T to one hour and thirty-five minutes from more than twelve hours a few years earlier. In 1909 a Model T cost $950, already well down from the $2,000 or $3,000 for a car a decade earlier that had restricted it to being a plaything for the wealthy. In that year Ford sold an impressive 12,000 cars. But by 1916 he had reduced the price of a Model T to $360. Nearly 600,000 of them rolled off his assembly lines. By the 1920s he was selling more than 2 million cars a year.[39]

Ford reduced radically the amount of labor per car. But where giant factories in the nineteenth century employed at most one thousand workers or so, astonishing enough at the time, these new mass-production factories employed twenty thousand workers and more in a single facility. Ford also paid his workers well, famously doubling the wage for many of them in one day in 1913 to an unheard-of five dollars an hour. Like most successful American entrepreneurs, Ford was also an aggressive marketer, the first to establish a nationwide network of dealerships.[40]

Helped by rapid electrification in the 1920s, many consumer products were soon made cheaply and reliably on Fordist production lines, including washing machines, refrigerators, radios, telephones, and phonographs. The economy boomed in the 1920s, growing, as we have seen, on average by 6 percent a year between 1922 and 1928. Productivity, as we have also noted, leaped ahead at 4 percent a year, in one year rising by 9 percent. Though the growth in real wages slowed early in the century, by 1930 wages had about doubled. By then 60 percent of American households owned a car, most had electricity, and a quarter of them even had an electric washing machine. A genuine middle class arose. So did warnings about the dangers of a consumer society.[41]

Mass production was growing more sophisticated as well. Companies learned to take advantage of "economies of scope." A manufacturer could produce similar or related products in the same facilities at low costs. Businesses could also take advantage of their already efficient distribution and marketing channels by selling related, or even some unrelated, products through them. DuPont diversified from chemicals into dyes, paints, and film products. General Electric and Westinghouse, both originally makers of power equipment, now manufactured and sold home appliances. General Motors introduced five different car models in different price ranges, undermining Ford's outdated obsession with making only one car as efficiently as possible. As had been the case for the preceding fifty years, the primary advantage of a vast marketplace was that it stimulated the growth of an expanding network of other advantages not available to other countries.

Another example of this tendency of advantages to build upon one another was the continual discovery of new natural resources. Coal deposits found in the 1830s supplied energy to our first factories. A half century later, the discovery of the Mesabi iron-ore range gave American steelmakers a decided advantage over their international rivals. Vast oil reserves brought kerosene lamps to the average American home, and eventually made driving cars far cheaper for the average American than for his counterpart in Europe or Japan.[42]

Though our mass-production industries consumed these natural resources intensively, we did not run out of them as so many had warned. Fast economic growth provided such high financial incentives to find new reserves that Americans kept discovering more. After nearly half a century of leadership in mass production, as late as 1913 we were still the world's leading producer of natural gas and petroleum, copper, coal, iron ore, lead, tungsten, and even salt. In bauxite, we were number two only after France.[43] Significant new discoveries of key minerals were made in America well into the twentieth century and in some cases right into the 1950s, keeping prices lower for many of these natural resources than in most other countries and giving our mass-production industries a further advantage. After World War II, global prosperity created similar incentives for other nations to make discoveries of such resources around the world.

=

So well established were American mass-production and distribution companies that most of them survived the Great Depression intact. By the end of World War II, mass production was more important to the American economy than ever before. In 1917 the largest 278 industrial companies, almost all of them mass producers, accounted for more than 25 percent of the output of goods. In 1947 the 200 largest companies accounted for 47 percent of output.[44]

After World War II, America's mass-production industries grew even more dominant. Although we now made 50 percent of the world's manufactured goods, it was the rapid growth of domestic markets that drove mass-production and distribution companies to play an even larger role in the national economy. Many regional and suburban markets were to be as big as the national market had been before the war. New technologies that came out of World War II resulted in commercial products such as computers, plastics, pharmaceuticals, and jet engines that were also adaptable to mass-production or distribution methods.[45]

New economies of scale in marketing on network television were another source of growth. TV commercials were too expensive for manufacturers of narrowly targeted products. You needed large sales volume to amortize the costs. For the successful mass-market product, however, from corn flakes to cars, the cost of reaching an individual consumer with a sales message fell dramatically. The three networks would eventually reach 90 percent of the audience. Again, these were advantages of scale that foreign nations could not yet duplicate.

As production, distribution, and marketing economies of scale increased over these years, productivity rose rapidly, even though service industries accounted for more of our GDP, rising from about one third of GDP in the late nineteenth century, to about two thirds of GDP after World War II, to 75 percent of GDP by the 1970s, and to more than 80 percent today. Service industries, which include everything from department stores, banks, insurance companies, railroads, planes, and federal and local governments to restaurants and laundries, are typically more labor-intensive than manufacturing industries and therefore usually less productive. But productivity in services in general rose in the past, not as rapidly as in manufacturing, but considerably faster than it does now. Large, efficient firms dominated many such industries, including wholesaling, retailing, banking, insurance, and transportation, in which economies of scale and scope could be employed. The productivity of the satellite companies that serviced the mass-production and distribution giants also rose comparatively rapidly as they increased their own efficiency by taking advantage of the size, stability, and streamlined needs of their giant customers. Data that compare manufacturing and service productivity are not reliable, but it is fairly clear that only in the past two decades has productivity growth in services fallen so sharply.[46] The widely discussed shift to a services economy, then, does not account for our overall decline in productivity. Over the past few decades the shift itself would have reduced productivity by no more than .2 percent or .3 percent a year. Rather, the productivity gains of the huge services sector have slowed to a virtual crawl where once they had risen rapidly.[47]

So rich were we over these years that our economy could also support many specialized, low-volume industries, as well as industries ranging from those that made individually crafted products to education, publishing, and the arts that were not readily amenable to mass-production methods. The costs of producing these goods and services, which are comparatively labor-intensive, typically rose faster than costs in industries where economies of scale could be adopted more easily. But as long as we were growing rapidly, and people were making more money, we could afford the costly diversity. These low-productivity activities are now under increasing pressure as economic growth has slowed.

=

This, then, is what America had. Starting with the American monopoly over a vast marketplace, the advantages of mass production were compounded over and over again—in distribution, advertising, management, and other services, in the discovery of raw materials, and hands-on experience. No other country had access to such a market, and therefore no other country enjoyed the added benefits to such a degree. Europe, with smaller markets, tariffs, wars, and high transportation costs, was inefficient by comparison.

Mass production required big companies, and it was big business that led growth in America. While Americans were justifiably suspicious of the market power of big corporations and the conformity they demanded of their workers and customers, these companies were best able to exploit the economies of scale and scope that were the foundation of our exceptional growth. They had other partially redeeming attributes as well. Giant, comparatively stable mass-production companies generally invested in expensive capital equipment and new technology aggressively. Andrew Carnegie, for example, raised his investment in his steel company by ten times between 1880 and 1900.[48] Companies such as Kodak began investing formally in R&D as early as the 1880s.[49] After World War II, giant private corporations, including AT&T (Bell Labs), IBM, and Westinghouse, made many of our most important scientific breakthroughs. Large companies also generally created huge, permanently employed workforces. They paid comparatively high wages. It was from these companies that labor unions won their biggest gains and influenced wage-setting across the rest of the nation. For all our romantic attachment to small companies, studies show that large companies on average provided better employee benefits, were often more innovative, and usually invested more aggressively.[50]

But by the 1950s the "doctrine" of mass production was reaching its zenith in America. Among American businessmen, traditional mass production was thought of as a high point in production techniques that could not be exceeded.[51] The key objective of every well-managed business was unalloyed Fordism, to be the largest producer, distributor, or retailer in the industry in order to achieve the lowest costs. "If cost per unit decreases predictably with the number of units produced," wrote *Fortune* magazine, summarizing the business thinking of the day, "then the manufacturer with the most units should have the lowest marginal costs. To make more widgets than anyone else, though, one presumably has to sell more widgets, that is, have the largest share of the widget market. The market share leader can underprice competitors by virtue of its lower costs. . . . Eventually, market shares will stabilize, nobody new will want to enter the business because of Numero Uno's advantage, and the big guy can reap his reward."[52]

As usual, the three giant auto companies set the standard. Every time sales volume for a particular car model doubled, the rule of thumb was that the cost of manufacturing each car fell by 25 percent. In 1955 six models made by GM, Ford, and Chrysler accounted for 80 percent of all the cars sold in America, some 5.5 million of them. The production runs of some of these cars exceeded 1 million a year.[53] The proportion of U.S. manufacturing output of the nation's 200 largest industrial companies, essentially mass-production companies, rose to 61 percent by 1968. Maybe the most remarkable achievement of mass production was that of the 278 largest industrial companies in 1917, 264 were still in operation in 1967 either independently or as part of another company.[54]

But as America's international rivals gained access to our vast marketplace the great advantages that we had enjoyed for more than a century eroded quickly. Competition increased around the world. Moreover, these competitors were highly innovative. They successfully challenged the single-minded mass-production doctrine just when it had seemed inviolable. We had taken our rate of growth for granted for so long, attributing it mostly to our special characteristics as a people, that it is difficult for us even now to imagine that our exceptionalism may not be permanent.

Chapter 3

WHAT WE LOST

In the 1950s and 1960s it hadn't occurred to any of us that our rate of economic growth could slow down. We were the country with the most money to invest, with the best-educated workers, and with the best technology by far. We were told that only we could make giant computers and commercial jets. So optimistic were we that the celebrated forecast mentioned in Chapter 1 that productivity would grow at 4 percent a year indefinitely was taken seriously.[1] Had that occurred, we could have afforded a rising defense budget, higher Social Security benefits, universal health care, and even a new war on poverty, and the federal government could still have cut taxes and its budget would have been in substantial surplus. As far as I can find, no expert anticipated how rapidly other nations would catch up with us as free trade, lower transportation costs, and world peace gave them access to our unique marketplace and enabled them to build larger, unified markets of their own.

America led the efforts toward free trade. The international consensus against tariffs and other trade barriers after World War II was the consequence of harsh historical lessons. The failure to establish a free-trade regimen or any sort of broad economic coordination after World War I was widely seen as a principal cause of the economic misery that set the stage for the rise of Hitler and, thus, World War II. The General Agreement on Tariffs and Trade that resulted established an ambitious schedule of cuts in protective tariffs, quotas, and other trade-inhibiting practices among about two dozen participating nations. The Bretton Woods agreement of 1944 stabilized international currencies by anchoring them to the strong U.S. dollar, thus facilitating trade across borders. The Common Market was formed in 1957 by leading European countries, sharply reducing trade barriers among its members and producing a free-trade zone about the same size in terms of population if not yet as wealthy as America's.[2]

As trade barriers fell worldwide trade expanded more than fivefold in twenty years.[3] Most countries, including the United States, benefited from the expanding commerce. As free-trade theorists promised, each country more or less specialized in what it made best. In particular, advanced nations now had a marketplace in which to exploit fully economies of scale and scope. As mass production and distribution spread, the United States was no longer the exception it had once been.

Free trade and lower transportation costs brought about by fast oceangoing ships of enormous size and growing air freight created a single worldwide market for natural resources as well. By the early 1960s the prices for raw materials had more or less equalized in most advanced countries. The increasing ability to sell raw materials economically from almost anywhere in the world also encouraged the discovery and development of new resources everywhere, especially as foreign economies grew wealthier. In 1910, for example, Europe and the United States had almost all the known iron-ore reserves in the world. Today, iron-ore reserves in Asia and South America exceed ours by a wide margin. Similarly, America had by far the largest oil reserves in 1913; by the 1960s America's reserves were a small fraction of the world's supply. In fact, America became a net importer of many minerals and other natural resources over these years.[4]

But raw materials had also become a less important component of manufactured products. New, lighter, often synthetic materials replaced the older raw materials in many products. As products became more complex the purchase of more sophisticated production equipment as well as such services as marketing, packaging, and specialized engineering became larger components of the cost of manufacturing than raw materials themselves. Raw materials accounted for 25 percent of GDP in 1900 and only 7 percent by 1970.[5]

There was no turning back any longer to a time when nations could go it alone. Even the American economy, which depended so much less on exports than other national economies did, grew more quickly than it otherwise would have done as international trade expanded. Meanwhile, the benefits of a vast market and cheap natural resources were no longer uniquely ours.

=

Until these changes took firm hold, the development of true mass-production industries among our overseas rivals had been spotty. All European producers were dependent on trade across borders to supplement their small domestic markets, but such trade was slow, often interrupted by war, and almost always restricted by tariffs, quotas, and poor transportation. While so-called heavy industries such as steel and machinery were well developed in Germany and several other countries, companies there were often devoted to comparatively specialized production. By contrast, the kinds of mass-production industries that thrived in America, especially in consumer products, typically made little headway overseas. In the late 1920s, for example, American cars accounted for 33 percent of world exports, while German cars accounted for less than 1 percent.[6]

But by the latter half of the 1950s these overseas economies were being transformed, using the U.S. mass-production industries as their model. The Japanese moved earliest and most effectively toward adopting mass production. By the 1960s, many major industries were also fully employing mass-production methods in Germany, France, Italy, and smaller European countries, their transformation actively supported by their respective governments. In these early years Japan and Europe had an additional competitive edge over the United States because their wages were still considerably lower than ours. Even as late as the 1960s, wages in Japan and Europe were only about 40 percent of ours on average.[7]

Mass production of such products as metals, autos and auto parts, consumer electronics, machinery, household appliances, and computers grew rapidly in Japan and in European nations. As a result, we lost our heretofore unchallenged dominance of worldwide exports as our share of total exports fell from 32 percent in 1955 to 18 percent in 1971. By then we were also importing more foreign-made goods. Our imports rose from about 3.5 percent of GDP in the early postwar years to about 6 percent by 1970. Some foreign products, of course, had already made deep forays into our markets. The percentage of foreign-made consumer electronics products bought by Americans, for example, rose from 4 percent in 1960 to 31 percent in 1970, led by a wave of Japanese transistor radios followed by television sets. Only a relative handful of foreign-made cars were sold in the United States in the early 1950s, but by 1970 they accounted for more than 15 percent of the market. U.S. imports of Japanese steel made similar gains. By 1971 we posted our first postwar trade deficit.[8]

With mass-production transformations fully under way, and worldwide trade unhindered and booming, Italy, France, and Germany showed annual rates of economic growth of 5 percent and 6 percent in the 1950s and 1960s, and Japan grew at more than 9 percent a year. In Japan, output per worker rose at a rate of 8 percent a year, and productivity in Germany and France rose by 6 percent and 5 percent a year, respectively. For many other European nations, productivity grew at 3.5 percent to 4 percent a year. At last, productivity levels in these countries converged with ours. Between 1950 and 1973, Japan's output per worker rose from 15 percent of America's level to 46 percent, Germany's from 30 percent to 64 percent, and France's from 40 percent of U.S. productivity to 70 percent.[9]

As America became less dominant in the world economy, the dollar could no longer serve as its anchor currency. In 1973 exchange rates were set free, and prices of goods traded in international markets became less predictable. The tripling of oil prices, also in 1973, jarred the economies of all advanced nations, and foreshadowed the long decline that began at that time. It is by now conventional wisdom to blame the high price of oil and floating currencies for at least part of the productivity slowdown of the past twenty years.

But despite their greater dependence on exports and worldwide trade, other advanced nations fared far better than we did in this new environment. Their productivity-growth rates generally slowed from the earlier postwar levels, but didn't fall nearly to America's low post-1973 rate of growth of less than 1 percent. Japan's rate fell from 7.5 percent a year to 3.5 percent, and Germany's and France's from roughly 5 percent or 6 percent to 3 percent a year. By the early 1980s, as inflation raised most other prices, the price of oil settled back toward its pre-crisis levels, eliminating it as an ongoing drag on economic growth. Yet America's unusual productivity slowdown persisted even as these problems came and went.[10]

Over the next twenty years, products from our newly energized rivals made deep inroads in our domestic markets, though wages paid in these nations now approached our own. By the mid-1980s, foreign autos accounted for 30 percent of all our sales. We lost almost our entire consumer electronics industry to foreign producers. Japanese producers upset our dominance in such traditional stalwarts as steel, machine tools, and a newer industrial product in which we were once the unrivaled leader, semiconductors. The American merchandise trade deficit rose dramatically, from $1.5 billion in 1971 to $30 billion in 1978. Exports were especially hurt by the rising dollar in the 1980s. By 1987, our trade deficit had risen to more than $150 billion.[11] By the end of the 1980s, the economies of these foreign rivals had grown so fast as to challenge our own. Both productivity and standards of living for some of our leading competitors rose to between 70 percent and 85 percent of ours.[12]

By the latter half of the 1970s mass production had also successfully spread to smaller Pacific Rim countries, including Hong Kong, Taiwan, Singapore, and South Korea, countries that still paid low wages. The products of these nations ranged from light assembled manufactures, such as toys and apparel, to increasingly sophisticated mass-produced goods, such as consumer electronics, semiconductors, and cars. An expanding circle of even lower-wage nations, from Mexico and other Latin American countries to Indonesia, Thailand, India, and China, had also begun to develop both basic manufacturing and full-fledged mass-production industries as well. They followed a pattern similar to their earlier counterparts in the Pacific Rim. Many of the original products in which they gained a competitive advantage, such as toys, pens, eyeglasses, apparel, and electronics components, required only simple assembly and production operations. But more quickly than most had anticipated, these countries were making headway in major mass-production industries, such as steel, glass, beer, autos, auto parts, and machinery, and in still more sophisticated industries such as computer chips. In the late 1970s, our imports from low-wage producers started to rise more quickly than those from the more advanced nations.[13] By 1990 about 36 percent of our imports were from nations whose wages were 50 percent or less than ours compared with only about 25 percent from such nations in 1978. For almost all of these lower-wage producers, selling to the American marketplace was an essential spur to economic takeoff.[14]

Overall, by the 1990s, foreign imports equaled 20 percent or more of what we manufactured in telecommunications equipment, computers, glass, turbines and generators, machine tools, semiconductors, aluminum, steel, textiles, ladies' garments, farm machinery, tires, toys, and sporting goods. Our imports of goods and services rose to more than 12 percent of

GDP. The merchandise trade deficit made a new record of some $166 billion in 1994, though the low dollar has given U.S. manufacturers, who some experts claim have become much more efficient, a significant advantage. Uncounted in these calculations are the markets we would have won over-seas for ourselves had rival economies not developed as rapidly as they did. The lost markets since the early 1970s have resulted in fewer jobs and lower wages for American workers, the abandonment of some industries, idle capacity in many others, and reduced capital investment overall.

=

But international competition alone cannot explain the de-gree to which our economy slowed down, our wages fell, or our investment flagged.[15] In my view, there is another sig-nificant factor. Traditional mass production has been trans-formed in the last two decades into a much more flexible but also more competitive system of manufacturing than before. Through new electronic machinery and the adoption of countless commonsense innovations on the factory floor, economies of scale have become less important. So-called flexible production now efficiently put out a greater variety of products in a single factory or even on a single assembly line at a reasonable cost, enabling manufacturers to target many smaller, specialized markets. There were parallel changes in service industries such as finance, distribution, and retailing, as products from banking services to specialty clothing be-

came more varied in order to reach targeted groups of consumers.[16]

This shift in production and distribution methods further
intensified competition. Once-standardized American markets became increasingly fragmented. As new products prolif-
erated, consumers became much more selective. Innovation
in products, production methods, and marketing became an
increasingly potent source of market share. Economies of
scale, market power, or other advantages of size such as fi-
nancing capability could no longer be depended on to give
firms an unassailable competitive advantage.

This flexibility opened markets not only to more foreign
producers but also to more domestic ones, often smaller companies. As a result, the tight lock big American business once
had on domestic industry weakened for the first time in more
than a century. On average, the size of an American firm fell
in the 1980s in terms of both sales and number of employees
after rising throughout the postwar period.[17] An IBM executive figured that in 1965, for example, his company had approximately 2,500 competitors in all its markets. By 1992 IBM
had some 50,000 competitors.[18] Large businesses were by no
means about to disappear from the landscape, but now in
order to compete they, too, had to become more flexible and
respond more quickly to rising competition.[19] As the power of
traditional big business receded, some of the key advantages
that a mass-production economy once afforded us declined—
namely, the high level of capital investment, organizational

efficiency, and the large, permanent workforce that stability and economies of scale once made possible. The new environment was more uncertain and produced lower rates of return, to which American business did not react well.

==

It was foreign manufacturers who originally led the way toward flexible production. To a degree, this was only natural. They were not as attached to our old thinking as we were, particularly the Fordist ways of doing business, which still emphasized selling a single standardized product to the largest market possible in order to ensure the lowest production costs. American business was also more or less trapped by huge investments sunk in traditional mass-production plants and equipment. Many American businessmen remained complacent. As late as 1978 Detroit's automakers insisted that the only serious advantage the Japanese manufacturers had over American carmakers was lower wages.[20] One reason foreign manufacturers penetrated our markets so easily, even as their wages rose, was that American companies were generally slow to adopt the new production methods.[21]

By the late 1970s Japanese automakers, for example, were able to manufacture high-quality cars with only fifty man-hours of labor compared with eighty for comparable American models. They could shift production from one model to another quickly and inexpensively, and add a variety of features to their products at less cost than we could. New production methods also enabled them to reduce defects in their cars dramatically at low cost. In all, the Japanese manufacturers could make a substantial profit manufacturing 500,000 high-quality cars over the life of a single model, while American manufacturers were still committed to making 2 million to 2.5 million over the life of a single model.[22] This flexibility was the consequence of new electronic equipment and significant if more mundane changes in handling inventories and reorganizing production lines, which resulted in leaner, more efficient, ultimately cheaper production. Flexible and lean production went hand in hand.[23]

With these tools at their disposal, Japanese car manufacturers introduced more new models each year and discarded their old models sooner. In 1955 there were only 30 basic car models on the world market, excluding the many minor models differentiated only by small variations in design and extra equipment. Of these, 25 were made in America, and the rest in Europe. By the late 1980s there were more than 140 basic models, and the Japanese made 58. Detroit, which at last had begun to adopt new production methods, was making only 50.[24]

Many foreign manufacturers, from steelmakers to consumer electronics makers, either emulated the Japanese automakers or developed similar innovations on their own. In Europe manufacturers learned how to make seemingly customized products in the factory cheaply and competitively. Their new methods, typically using the latest electronic machinery, combined the cost savings of large mass-production runs with craftsmanlike attention to detail and quality. In

Italy and Germany, and also in France, Spain, Sweden, and Denmark, smaller companies made a variety of innovative, well-crafted products, from home appliances to farm tools, ceramics, and textiles, which quickly penetrated American markets.[25]

At last American companies got into the fray. Not only our auto companies but other makers of durable goods brought out a growing variety of refrigerators, washers, and personal computers, among many other products. In 1970, only about 1,000 new food products were introduced in America. By 1985, there were 5,000, and by 1993, 13,000, mostly from American companies. Among new beverages alone, including gourmet coffees, soft drinks, juices, beers, and bottled waters, the number of new-product introductions rose from 123 in 1970 to 1,845 in 1993. The number of new-product introductions of such items as household supplies, health and beauty aids, foil and tissue paper, and tobacco rose nearly fifteenfold from 324 in 1970 to nearly 4,700 in 1993.[26]

American companies led the introduction of a parade of new computer software and video games, as well as toys and other children's products, as more movies, records, CDs, and other entertainment products were produced each year. The variety of fashionable apparel available at modest prices, now often manufactured in Asia, expanded rapidly. New cable TV networks took market share from the original big three networks, whose percentage of the audience fell from roughly 90 percent to nearly 60 percent between 1970 and 1990. To a lesser but nevertheless significant degree, the markets for industrial products also became more specialized and fragmented. In America specialty steelmakers, for example, had been outperforming the traditional mass producers for years. Chemical companies generally remained innovative and oriented toward developing new products.[27]

A climate of competition was created that eventually went well beyond flexible-production methods themselves as consumers responded enthusiastically to more choice. Service industries were widely affected as new information-gathering technology, including point-of-sale computers, enabled retailers, marketers, financial institutions, and others to pinpoint specific groups of consumers and tailor services for them.[28] Specialty retail stores such as the Gap took business from the department stores by targeting their markets and changing inventory rapidly. Warehouse-type chains, such as Wal-Mart and Toys "R" Us, and nationwide price clubs intensified competition while making a wider variety of products available to consumers at affordable prices. The use of such narrowly targeted advertising vehicles as direct marketing, including telemarketing, increased rapidly. The cable TV networks and new radio stations also provided advertisers with ways to target markets more narrowly than they once could. Finally, the movement of capital became much more fluid, as the money available for investment traveled quickly from place to place, enabling competitors to enter markets more easily.

=

Rising intensity of competition can enhance economic growth greatly by forcing businesses to innovate, invest more, and keep prices low. Without significantly more choice in products, consumer demand may weaken, which may have been happening in America as early as the 1960s, so satiated was the American consumer with the standardized products of mass production.[29]

But such competitiveness can go too far. Ultimately, flexible production and the growing demand by consumers for variety has proved costly. While the new flexible and lean production methods had at first lowered manufacturing costs and raised productivity, some long-standing advantages of economies of scale were lost. The additional costs of producing smaller batches of products had merely been reduced, not eliminated. Once the initial productivity gains were made, it was still usually more expensive to make ten different products for one hundred thousand customers than it would have been to make only one, though the financial penalty had been lowered.[30]

This was also true for distribution and marketing. Where once 90 percent of the TV audience could be reached by advertising on only three networks, for example, an advertiser by the late 1980s now had to use six to ten different traditional and cable networks. According to one study, marketing costs of a typical brand-name consumer product sold in America rose from 25 percent of the wholesale price in 1980 to 50 percent today.[31] Reforms in manufacturing and even in services might raise productivity rapidly at first, but after that, ongoing gains in productivity were typically harder to achieve in an intensely competitive economy of flexible production and fragmented markets than in an economy dominated by traditional highly standardized mass-production products.

As flexible production and fragmenting markets spread, profit margins and rates of return on investment fell consistently in most advanced nations between the 1960s and 1980s. The new competitiveness also added to the uncertainty of doing business. Fragmenting markets were more volatile and unpredictable than standardized mass markets had been, and flexible production made it easier for more competitors to enter these industries. The typical product introduction became increasingly risky as good product ideas came and went quickly. In traditional mass production, the payoff for a dollar invested in a bigger plant or distribution facility was comparatively certain; the business would enjoy predictable costs savings from further economies of scale. Such stability encouraged giant companies to invest aggressively not only in capital equipment but also in R&D. But the payoff for a dollar invested in an entirely new product or technology in an environment of flexible production and fragmented markets was less certain, especially when distribution and marketing muscle counted for less than they once did. This is one reason that capital investment flagged.[32]

By the 1990s even Japanese manufacturers had to face the consequences of the competitiveness they had done so much to create. Low profit margins and returns on investment forced Japanese auto and consumer electronics makers to reduce the number of new products they offered, as well as the number of variations on their older products.[33] Many smaller, specialized European companies in everything from textiles to farm tools were doing less well also. European and Japanese manufacturers in general were busy cutting costs, reducing investment, and even firing workers as recessions overtook their economies in the early 1990s.[34] The low dollar made selling in the United States even tougher for foreign producers.

But rising competition from foreign firms, flexible production, and fragmenting markets had disrupted American business much earlier, and our reaction to it was generally more damaging.[35] There were several reasons for this. First, wed to our Fordist tradition, we generally have not had as much faith in the new production methods, did not use them well at first, and maybe for the most part still don't, which is partly why we have been slow to invest in them. Instead, our companies typically emphasized cutting costs to keep prices low, rather than investing in new production methods. Studies show that even when American firms bought new computerized equipment, they typically used it to raise volume and reduce per-unit costs rather than produce smaller, more customized batches of products as the Japanese and Europeans were doing.[36]

Second, because of the attention American businesses traditionally pay to profits, they were reluctant to invest in capital projects as rates of return fell. By contrast, though margins and returns were actually lower in Japan and Germany than in the United States, these nations kept investing liberally.[37] Third, with levels of unused capacity rising faster in America than in other countries, companies with idle capacity were understandably reticent about investing. Fourth and, as noted, maybe most important, rising business uncertainty affected America more than it did other countries because it represented a sharper change in the business environment. In general, we reduced capital investment more than other countries did in the face of the unfamiliar levels of risk, and even a rise in capital investment in 1993 and 1994 did not match the levels of the 1950s and 1960s, nor is it as yet certain that these higher rates of capital investment will be sustained. Net investment as a proportion of GDP rose to only about 3 percent of GDP in 1994 compared with 7 percent to 8 percent of GDP in the 1950s and 1960s.[38]

These tendencies were reinforced by Wall Street. Investors typically punished any drop in corporate profits or cash flow with lower stock prices, even those due to rising investment expenditures. Wall Street made matters worse by diverting available money to financial speculation that provided higher returns than the real economy did. First there were conglomerates in the 1960s, then hostile corporate takeovers in the 1970s, finally leveraged buyouts, eventually financed by junk bonds, in the 1980s, and most recently financial derivatives.

Overall, capital investment per worker rose by only 1.3 percent a year between 1973 and 1987 in America compared with 6.4 percent a year in Japan and 3.5 percent a year in Germany.[39] The consequences of falling rates of investment could be seen most starkly in R&D spending. In the early postwar years, we were easily the world's leader in R&D investment when both the Pentagon and large mass manufacturers spent freely on such projects. But by the late 1980s and early 1990s, German and Japanese nondefense R&D per capita was about 50 percent higher than America's.[40]

American business also cut labor costs more zealously than other nations did. To bolster sagging profits, American businesses in general slashed their workforces, farmed out work once done in-house to low-wage contractors both in America and abroad, and weakened the hold of labor unions as the number of organized workers in private industry fell from more than 35 percent of the workforce in the 1960s to about 11 percent now.[41] To become more flexible, even the best-managed companies replaced permanent workers with temporary and part-time ones who earned much less annually than permanent workers did. The number of temporary workers in America grew much faster than the permanent workforce.[42]

By the beginning of the 1990s the wages of American workers, measured in dollars (at record low levels), were among the lowest in the advanced world. Even in terms of purchasing power, American workers earned no more than workers did in Germany, France, or Norway, and only a little more than workers earned in a wide range of other nations.[43] This relative reduction in labor costs was welcomed in most quarters because it made us more cost-competitive with the rest of the world. But it remains to be seen whether wage cutting will provide permanent benefits to our economy. Most likely, such a competitive advantage is temporary. If they choose to, foreign competitors could ultimately match our lower wages, or if we grow rapidly again, we will have to raise our own. To match superior technological ability built up through persistent capital investment is much harder.[44]

So welcome were lower wages in business circles that it was widely overlooked that our internationally low wage levels were entirely unprecedented in our industrial history. Since the early nineteenth century, we had always paid the highest wages in the world.[45] Now, low wages effectively put a lid on the demand for goods and services, which in turn helped keep economic growth slow, and removed an important incentive for further capital investment.[46] The high cost of labor in the past was one of the key reasons that American businessmen had invested so much in improving technology ever since the nineteenth century.[47]

==

What America lost, then, was clear. First, we no longer had a vast, efficient marketplace and cheap natural resources to ourselves. American businesses and their employees were now for the first time subject to intense competition from new mass producers overseas. Second, conventional mass production and distribution, and their several considerable advantages, were in retreat domestically because of flexible production and fragmenting markets. Both of these factors served to reduce our capacity utilization rates and raise the costs of doing business for mass producers, which needed high volume to stay competitive. Third, American business reduced capital investment markedly in the face of rising competition, uncertainty, and falling returns. The further result was fewer jobs and lower wages, which slowed overall economic growth still more by reducing the demand for goods and services, and in turn further dampened returns on capital investment.

As the rate of capital investment fell, productivity growth slowed still more. As productivity growth slowed, business cut even more jobs or otherwise held down wages. Lower wages reduced the demand for goods and services another notch, lowering sales for business. Rates of return and profit margins were hurt even more. The incentives to invest were thereby reduced again, and the cycle started anew (see Figure 6 in the Appendix).

=

We don't know how these changes will play out over time. But despite the widespread claims that America has begun to reverse its fortunes it is likely that the factors that have made economies more competitive, reduced rates of return, and made productivity gains harder to achieve are here to stay. What improvements we have seen recently in productivity are almost entirely the consequence of the expansive phase of the business cycle, as we have noted. Even the recent gains in output per worker in services due to the increased use of computer technology are modest compared with the strides made in distribution, retailing, and marketing in the past when mass markets in everything from frozen meat to insurance to apparel replaced local markets serviced by small companies.

Consumers in the advanced nations will now probably continue to demand variety and quality. In fact, if firms try to raise margins by permanently shrinking the variety of products they offer, consumers may ultimately reduce their buying or look elsewhere for their products, which would slow economic growth in and of itself. The newfound consumer sovereignty has probably locked business into more intense competition indefinitely.

There will be ongoing pressure to keep costs low in order to remain flexible. Where once the mass-production giants were extraordinary job machines, providing millions of high-paying, secure jobs for only modestly educated workers, flexible producers will increasingly try to shave employment costs. Mass-production giants that once benefited from great organizational efficiency will probably increasingly farm out even more services once done in-house and join other companies in temporary alliances to undertake major projects, at less risk to all parties. But coordinating these efforts will probably cost more than they did when all such functions were done under one roof according to the highly honed principles of scientific management.[48]

Most important, innovations that do not depend on economies of scale and scope will increasingly become key competitive weapons, enabling many more companies to enter and leave markets, and even big companies will have to be much more flexible and innovative in order to compete. New technological advances, such as the so-called soft production systems pioneered by some American firms, that make manufacturing even more agile may enable us to introduce products still faster. But soft production will not win us a permanent advantage the way our innovations once did. Such innovations, as we have seen, are now quickly emulated or surpassed by our competitors, and they fragment markets still more. There is no evidence to suggest that future forms of production will re-create the special characteristics that economies of scale once offered American producers, especially the stability and relative certainty that gave rise to high levels of investment and permanent employment. The new conditions will be reinforced by ongoing economic expansion in developing nations that attract international capital and supply a constant flow of new, efficient, low-cost business competitors in all markets.

There will be slowdowns and temporary reversals of these trends, of course. As they recovered from the recession of the early 1990s, for example, some companies reverted to a search for greater economies of scale rather than pursue more flexibility and variety. Ford, for example, is trying to develop a world car—a single basic model that can be sold almost anywhere. But this is mostly a defensive strategy in stringent times.[49] Over time, markets will probably stay fragmented and consumers choosy. The payoff to capital investment will remain less certain than before, wages will remain under constant pressure, and companies will find it hard to retain large, stable, permanent workforces, dampening overall consumption. Slow economic growth will probably persist, not only in America but in other advanced nations. Even as America learns to compete aggressively, fast economic growth will not necessarily return, for we and our advanced competitors are probably all in the same slowing boat.

==

The gravest consequence of the retreat from traditional mass production and rising competitiveness for the United States has been the sharp reduction in the growth of middle-class jobs that do not require a higher education, most obviously in manufacturing. This is a significant break from past trends in job creation, one whose severity is even today still underestimated. Until the 1970s, gains in productivity never came at the expense of manufacturing jobs overall. Since the second half of the 1800s, industry always grew fast enough to create more manufacturing jobs than it lost through the application of new technologies. Even in the early post–World War II years, when the proportion of manufacturing workers fell from 33.7 percent of the workforce to

27.2 percent between 1950 and 1970, we nevertheless gained 4.1 million more manufacturing jobs than we lost.[50]

But beginning in the early 1970s we started to lose more manufacturing jobs than we created. Between 1970 and 1990, the total number of manufacturing jobs in America fell on balance by some three hundred thousand, the first such net loss in our industrial history. The proportion of manufacturing jobs in the workplace dropped sharply over this period to only 17.4 percent. Between 1990 and 1993, the number of lost manufacturing jobs rose dramatically to 1.3 million on balance. We regained only some three hundred thousand such jobs as the economic expansion continued into 1994 and early 1995. There is no hard evidence, however, that the loss of jobs to newer technologies had quickened since the early 1970s. New technologies had probably been replacing workers with machines at about the same steady pace since the end of World War II. Rather, the more rapid pace of job losses coincided with the rising competition from overseas and from flexible production and fragmenting markets at home. Had the creation of manufacturing jobs slowed at merely the same rate between 1970 and 1990 as in the preceding two decades, not only would manufacturing jobs not have been lost on balance, but an additional 4.6 million of them would have been created.[51]

The actual damage done since the early 1970s was more severe than the net loss of manufacturing jobs suggests. What new manufacturing jobs were created typically paid less and offered fewer benefits than the old ones. The average length of unemployment for laid-off workers increased, and many more had to jump from one part-time job to another. The lost manufacturing jobs at giant mass producers also reduced the number of good manufacturing jobs among the satellite companies that supplied them. Jobs were also lost and wages were cut at mass distributors, retailers, and marketers as fragmenting markets disrupted their businesses. When workers couldn't find manufacturing jobs, they typically had to settle for lower-paying jobs in such service industries as retailing and wholesaling, many of which now had to cut wage costs sharply in order to compete. Only a small minority advanced to the new higher-paying service jobs in finance, law, and marketing.[52] By the late 1980s the distribution of income had skewed significantly in favor of the top 20 percent or so of earners.

The consequences of slowing economic growth spread to the better service jobs as well. These jobs became scarcer in the recession of 1990–91 and white- and blue-collar workers were let go in equal numbers, something that had never happened in a recession before. Analysts found that, on average, the high salaries paid to skilled, educated workers had been falling for several years before the recession. Even a good education looked increasingly as if it would not protect workers from declines in earnings. The erosion of these jobs started later than it did in manufacturing partly because the stimulus of outsize federal and private borrowing contributed to a boom in medicine, real estate, financial services, and related industries such as law, which continued well after slow growth had affected the rest of the economy.[53]

Finally, of course, an increasing proportion of workers couldn't find jobs. The average unemployment rate climbed from 4.5 percent in the 1950s and 4.8 percent in the 1960s to 6.2 percent in the 1970s and 7.3 percent in the 1980s, and has averaged between 6 percent and 7 percent so far in the 1990s.[54] As many as one million Americans left the workforce entirely, and were no longer counted among the unemployed. Higher rates of unemployment could not be adequately explained, as some had tried to do, by the rising proportion of females and young workers in the workforce who typically had had higher rates of unemployment in the past, and entered and left the workforce more readily. By the latter half of the 1980s the proportion of these workers in the labor force was declining. Rather, there was a shortage of jobs, especially well-paying ones.

The standard of living for many Americans eroded over these years. The typical American family earned as much in 1993 as the typical American family did in 1973 largely because spouses went to work.[55] As middle-class jobs dissipated, the proportion of the population in poverty, many of whom held a full-time job, rose dramatically from 11 percent to 15 percent.[56] Finally, the symbol of America's social mobility, owning a home, was increasingly out of reach. The proportion of all those Americans under fifty-five who owned a home has fallen since 1973 for the first time ever, and for those under thirty-five, the prime home-buying group, ownership fell sharply.[57]

==

All advanced nations in the world are subject to the same competitive economic conditions that we have described above. An important difference, however, is that most other advanced nations have been accustomed to slower economic growth over the course of their histories and have learned to form functioning societies under circumstances where opportunity was not so ample or widespread as it has been for them in the post–World War II period, and where standards of living did not always rise inexorably.[58]

We have no such experience. Despite the many problems of the last two decades, few Americans, I think, have come to terms with the possibility that our prospects may have changed permanently. We remain a deeply optimistic country. One belief we harbor as a result is that if we simply reduce some costs of government and discard many government regulations, we can return to the rapid growth of our first and second frontiers and the many social blessings that accompanied them. But in the real world there is no returning. The conditions that created our unique history resulted from factors that we can't re-create: the original frontier, abundant natural resources, and a unique marketplace that produced a mass production revolution.

Even those Americans who are more realistic nevertheless cling to a stubborn faith in our ability to solve any problem. Over the past two decades we have as a nation turned from one proposed solution to another with confidence that this time we have found the answer, inevitably to be disappointed and forced to start our search again. As commendable as this habitual optimism may sometimes be, it distorts our perspective as a nation. We will next look in greater detail at the most commonly proposed solutions to our economic dilemma to see whether they address the central issues we have raised.

Chapter 4

Misplaced
Optimism

A merica's national creed is optimism. No other people in
the world has had reason to believe—as Americans have
had—that all of us can, at least in theory, improve our standard of living, or that at the very least each generation will do
better than the previous one. "As nature and experience justified optimism, the American was incurably optimistic," wrote
the historian Henry Steele Commager.[1] Faith in an ever better future sustained the ambition, hard work, and great
achievements of generations of Americans. So it is not surprising that we celebrate our optimism as an obvious virtue.
"We have nothing to fear but fear itself," "the power of positive thinking," "Boost, don't knock," "Yes, you can," "I'll do it
my way"—these are the expressions of our secular religion.
Most of us are ashamed not to be optimistic. "I did not come

to my pessimism easily," a *New York Times* reporter felt obliged to apologize in an article on prospects for peace in the Middle East. "I was from Minnesota, where America's innate optimism seems acute."[2]

For all our recent economic disappointments, both national and personal, I think most Americans still believe that someone or something will come along to make the economy right—an expert, an economist, a scientist, an inventor, even a politician or religious leader. In the fall of 1994, for example, while commentators widely reported that Americans were disillusioned by the political process, a broad-based survey found that 68 percent still believed we could "always" solve our problems and 63 percent agreed that there were no limits to our growth.[3] This optimism may explain why we have been so quick to embrace the variety of explanations offered by experts for the economy's weakness, explanations that invariably suggest that America's problems can sooner or later be fixed. Over the years, such explanations have blamed, among other factors, the oil price increases that began in 1973, the inflation that followed, and the high dollar in the early 1980s. Today oil prices are fairly low and stable compared with the prices of other commodities, inflation in general has subsided to a manageable rate, and the dollar has been trading at record-low levels for many years. Yet our economic dilemma remains. The suggested remedies include increasing the flexibility and competitiveness of our businesses, raising our savings rate, balancing the budget, improving our education, and developing new markets for our goods overseas. As we shall see, these remedies, helpful as some of them may be, do not address our core problems, either. Not even our faith that technological progress will inevitably sustain fast growth is any longer as warranted as it once was as economic circumstances change. Because we probably have more faith in technology than in anything else, we should examine it first.

==

I doubt that anything fires the American imagination more than the promise of technology. We customarily think of our industrial history as the saga of wondrous inventions that made our economy great and our people prosperous. As schoolchildren we memorized the string of inventions of the industrial revolution, and even some economic historians sometimes fall into the trap of explaining our economic growth largely in terms of these great breakthroughs, from the cotton gin to the reaper, the steam engine, the railroads, electricity, the car, and the computer.[4] Thus, we assume that similar scientific and technological breakthroughs will come along to stimulate our economic renewal. As often as not, it seems to me, when you suggest that the growth rate may not again reach its former heights, you are refuted by your listener with yet another example of a new technological breakthrough to prove the contrary.

This unrealistic view of technological development is understandable. The United States was born during the first stages of the scientific revolution, when the world seemed orderly and societies could turn that order to their advantage, a faith nowhere more evident than in America. "Abounding harvests of scientific discovery have been garnered by numberless inquisitive minds and the wildest forces of nature have been taught to become the docile helpmates of man," wrote the preeminent American historian of his time, George Bancroft, in 1882.[5]

Over the next century our faith in technology was strengthened even more by rapid economic growth. A popular government paper published in 1945 about the war's many technological breakthroughs was called *Science, the Endless Frontier.*[6] The title tells us a lot about ourselves. As if in answer to Frederick Jackson Turner's concerns, the technologies that led to the computer, plastics, wonder drugs, and jet travel, among other valuable innovations, were now seen as our new frontier, and moreover a frontier without limit. Today, we assume that everything from robotics to biotechnology, personal computers, interactive telecommunications, and the so-called information superhighway will prove the second coming of a miraculous breakthrough, like the railroads, the car, and electricity in the past.

But no matter how revolutionary new technological breakthroughs may be, what matters most is how well an economy can exploit them. The telegraph did not make the Australian bush as rich as the American West, nor did the railroads in nineteenth-century India make Calcutta into a Chicago. The railroads were important to American economic development, but not as important as the mass market they helped to create, which in turn stimulated the construction of still more railroads. Robert Fogel, a Nobel Prize–winning economic historian, has convincingly shown that had America developed a system of waterways and canals to create a nationwide marketplace instead of the railroads, the economic results would have been almost as good.[7] It was the burgeoning American marketplace more than a particular means of transport that made the crucial difference. Similarly, we exploited electricity more rapidly than other countries did because our mass-production giants could make such efficient use of the new source of power and because of the spreading demand for electricity by consumers who bought in huge numbers the new, mass-produced electrical goods, such as refrigerators and phonographs, that were priced low enough to be widely affordable.[8]

By comparison, today's best production technologies are increasingly fungible. Many countries now share, as we have seen, the advantageous economic environment that we once had to ourselves. The benefits of learning by doing, hands-on experience, and mass marketing and distribution, among others, have become common property among advanced economies, so that no nation can count on holding the lead indefinitely in new production technologies and management practices. Though our manufacturers still make important competitive innovations, and trial and error and learning by doing will still matter to a degree, leadership in industrial technologies will in the foreseeable future be highly competitive and widely distributed.[9]

Moreover, the technologies that underlie many of our

fastest-growing industries, including computers and software, aerospace, chemicals, scientific instruments, electric genera- tors, and telecommunications, are increasingly scientifically based, making them inherently more subject to competition than were the older, largely mechanical production technolo- gies, which depended more on hands-on experience and the advantages of scale conferred by a large marketplace.[10] New technologies are becoming more important to the older-line industries as well, such as automobiles, steel, and machine tools. Highly trained scientists and technicians everywhere from Silicon Valley to Asia and India are in constant contact about the latest advances in their fields, all of them increas- ingly able to translate technological advances from a techni- cal journal or electronic mail into an industrial advantage in their own countries, often at relatively low labor and produc- tion costs. The volume of new patents registered by citizens and institutions of other nations is now almost equal to our own, for example, and the six leading Asian nations have pro- duced more scientists and engineers than Europe, the United States, and Canada combined.[11] As we know, Japan, Germany, and several other nations now spend much more than we do per capita on nondefense R&D.[12] Such leading American companies as Motorola and Oracle have established com- puter software design operations as far away as India, and en- gineers are increasingly homegrown technicians who no longer have to be flown into countries like Malaysia from America and other advanced nations.[13]

The rapid penetration by Japan into the high-technology industries cited above shows how competitive the market can be and how vulnerable our early lead in these industries has been. According to the National Science Foundation, Japan's share of worldwide high-technology exports has risen from 18 percent to 28 percent of the world market since 1980, while the U.S. share has fallen from 40 percent to 36 percent. Developing nations, especially on the Pacific Rim, are starting to penetrate these markets more rapidly as well.[14] Because these high-technology industries are typically growing twice as fast as traditional manufacturing industries, experts encourage America to shift its resources as quickly as possible into these industries. But to replace completely our traditional manufacturing industries with only the fast-growing high-technology industries would require us to sell all the high-technology products that are now bought in the world today, and then some, about four times what we now make.[15]

In fact, rather than opening a lead in high-technology industries over other nations, as so many experts argue we should, it is more likely that we will have to work harder and invest more just to retain our current market shares. Even though we are still the leader in some of these key industries, including software, computer networking, computer chips, biotechnology, and pharmaceuticals, and a handful of our companies have broken ground in new flexible technologies, the transferability of high technology suggests that we will probably not retain it as easily or for as long as we once retained our lead in traditional mass-production industries. For us to compete in this technologically competitive world will require still more well-trained scientists and technicians, higher levels of investment, and a business environment that encourages risk-taking—all of which will become more difficult to achieve if our economy continues to grow slowly. In some key industries the rate of return on R&D has fallen.[16]

Complicating matters even more, today's companies, unlike traditional mass-production companies in our past, can no longer easily afford to undertake expensive research in search of breakthroughs in science that can soon be exploited by competing companies as well. Such scientific research in general cannot itself be patented. Only commercial products can. With both private corporations and public institutions more cautious about the R&D investment they now undertake, the development of such scientific "public" goods, so important to high-technology companies, is threatened.[17] Science and technology will surely continue to advance around the world, but it is a mistake to assume that the U.S. economy will automatically benefit from new technologies to the degree it once did, especially if our economy continues to grow slowly. The most rapidly growing, efficient economies will exploit more of the best existing technologies, and such rich economies, with ample funds to invest, will develop more of the advanced technologies that will allow them to stay ahead. Technological breakthroughs, no matter how large, no longer automatically confer even semipermanent leads on those who make them; the competition is now ongoing and intense, returns are short-lived, and outcomes more uncertain.

==

As we have seen, flexible production has swept the advanced industrial world. European manufacturers have adeptly used electronics and other new manufacturing techniques to make craftlike industries such as ceramics, apparel, and textiles much more productive than they once were. Older industries, from autos to metals, have been revitalized in Japan and now in the United States. Retailers have learned to turn over what they carry in inventory much more quickly in response to shifting market tastes and to target smaller segments of the market. Banks and insurance companies offer many more products than they once did.

Many widely read writers assume that with flexible production and distribution, American business will resume fast economic growth. For "conservative" visionaries, such as George Gilder and John Naisbitt, the greater variety of products made possible by flexible production and distribution will provide a new stimulus for America's individualism, entrepreneurialism, and competitiveness.[18] For "liberal" visionaries like Alvin Toffler and such "liberal" scholars as Michael Piore and Charles Sabel these new techniques can make us more productive by encouraging greater use of each worker's talents, more trust and cooperation between management and workers, and a more creative business environment in general.

The best-selling book *The Virtual Corporation,* by William H. Davidow and Michael S. Malone, anticipates that most of us will someday work more or less on our own, doing what we do best, and making an individually tailored product for every customer, with no limit to personal creativity or talent.[19]

For all this Jeffersonian appeal, however, flexible production and distribution have not yet produced the gigantic gains in productivity that mass production provided when it was first adopted. While there is less fat in all production methods these days, the new techniques, as we noted, have for the most part so far merely reduced but not eliminated the higher costs of flexibility and shorter production runs. Similarly, widely heralded new marketing and distribution techniques in traditional services—from cash machines that replace bank tellers to the computer networks that replace office workers to the computerized point-of-sale tracking of retail inventories—have not compensated entirely for the cost of servicing fragmenting markets. As a result, the growth of productivity in services, despite the hopes of industry, remains much slower than it once was. Estimates suggest that it is rising at about half a percent a year compared with between 1 percent and 2 percent a year, and at times even faster, in the past.[20]

Even if such new techniques as soft production make flexible production cheaper still,[21] the greater competitiveness they foster will continue to raise the level of uncertainty and instability in many industries, in many cases to levels that are probably detrimental to rapid growth as rates of return are reduced, investment becomes riskier, and highly paid, permanent workforces are harder to sustain. Consumer electronics companies, where lean production has enabled companies to turn out new products every year, have seen profits fall to zero on average. Some experts believe that an adequate level of investment in new electronics products is no longer being maintained. In the 1960s, for example, when most of the important breakthroughs in TV technology were made, RCA and Zenith spent on average two dollars a TV set on R&D. Now, profits for TV manufacturers are negligible.[22] Computer-industry profit margins are now so thin that R&D may be slighted there, too. "It is not clear that the fundamental research done by IBM in the 1950s and 1960s would have been economically possible in the more competitive environment [that began in] the 1970s," concludes a study done by the management consulting firm McKinsey and Company.[23] As noted, Japanese auto companies have been cutting back since the early 1990s on the variety of models they once made because of falling profit margins. Highly regarded technology companies that are considered models for the future, such as Silicon Graphics, boast that only half of their workers are now permanent employees. Their ultimate objective is to make the workforce even more flexible by hiring workers only when they are needed.[24]

In the twenty years that flexible production has been widely adopted in the advanced world, the rate of productivity growth in the sixteen richest nations fell on average by nearly half, to 2.3 percent a year since the early 1970s, compared with 4.5 percent a year between the end of World War

II and 1973.[25] Other factors, of course, have contributed to slowing economic growth around the world over these twenty years—such as higher oil prices, fluctuating exchange rates, maturing technologies, and a rising demand for lower-productivity services among all advanced countries. But the advantages of flexible production have been too modest to compensate for them. There was no such slowdown in overall productivity growth two centuries ago as old ways of producing goods were discarded in favor of mass production. Quite the contrary, the pace of overall productivity growth quickened.

Nor can we be certain that American business will be as good at flexible production as our international rivals. There are examples where American manufacturers have excelled, of course. But survey after survey shows that the more ambitious plans to restructure companies in recent years have not met expectations for up to two thirds of the companies that have implemented them. Experts like Robert Hayes, a management professor at Harvard Business School, say American companies still have a considerable way to go. "After all, the Japanese started this thirty years ago," he says. "We started it only ten years ago."[26] Given our historical record, it is likely that American business will in general learn to compete well. But we should also keep in mind that most businessmen in England were never very enthusiastic about altering their old managerial habits in favor of large-scale, American-style mass production.[27] What success American business has had in selling goods internationally in the 1990s has, so far at least, benefited greatly from low labor costs and record-low levels of the dollar that keep U.S. exports relatively cheap. In this environment it is difficult to determine how truly competitive we have become. The rapid fall in the value of the dollar in early 1995 may have been a warning that we have not come as far as some of us like to think we have.

Flexible production and more intense competition are almost certainly here to stay, and American corporations will have to be as lean and flexible as any of their international rivals in order to compete in what is now clearly a worldwide market for both consumer and producer goods and services, as well as for natural resources. Productivity can grow in this environment, but this is not to say that it can grow as quickly as it once did. We tend to assume in America that change always means advancement, because in our history it usually has. But to claim that flexible production and distribution will in themselves create a productivity revolution in manufacturing and services as great as mass production and mass distribution once did requires a leap of faith that our economic experience doesn't yet justify.

=

Another presumed cause of our economic decline is that we don't save enough. Our savings rate has fallen from 8 percent and 9 percent in the 1960s and 1970s to 4 percent and less in the 1980s and 1990s, largely as the result of slow economic growth. Individuals have had to dip into savings to supplement their stagnating or falling incomes. Reduced savings, in turn, leaves less money for capital investment, and forces up interest rates as the demand for capital threatens to exceed supply. The federal budget deficit—or negative savings—adds to the problem as excessive government borrowing also reduces savings available for capital investment, forcing us among other things to import expensive capital from abroad. The result, according to this view, has been the low rate of capital investment that has prevailed for the last two decades. The proposed remedy, therefore, is to raise our rate of savings and cut the federal deficit.

No doubt, higher levels of savings and a lower federal deficit would stimulate growth over a long enough period of time, but the evidence suggests that the slowdown in capital investment over the past twenty years has been caused more by the lack of opportunity to profit in a slow-growing economy than by the dearth of savings. For two decades, rising international competition and the advance of flexible production have left American businesses with high levels of unused capacity and growing confusion about what to invest in. Our existing businesses did not provide, or the managers did not perceive, enough opportunity to invest profitably what capital they already had. Government data show that the productivity of capital—the amount of output produced by a dollar of investment—has risen very slowly since 1973. Another measure known as multifactor productivity—the productivity of labor and capital combined—has risen at a rate of only .3 percent a year since 1973, compared with 2.2 percent a year between 1948 and 1973.[28] In such an economy, more savings or a cut in the federal deficit would almost certainly not have induced significantly more capital investment, and at times may even have dampened it by reducing the immediate demand for goods and services.[29] Cutting budget deficits too rapidly could well ensure that the rate of growth will remain slow and investment opportunities scarcer than they would otherwise be.

Nor should we presume that more savings would have brought our interest rates down significantly. America's high interest rates over these years were probably caused more by investors' fear of inflation than by the low rate of savings or high federal deficits, except insofar as growing federal deficits are themselves inflationary. Investors are less willing to hold securities that pay low interest rates if inflation promises to reduce the purchasing power of their future stream of income. Despite the receding federal deficit, for example, real interest rates (nominal rates less inflation) have fallen only slightly from around 6 percent in the 1980s to 5 percent in 1994. Real interest rates historically have averaged only about 3 percent.[30]

If our economic potential does improve in coming years, a higher rate of savings may be more important to our economy than it has been in the recent past. Under these circumstances, we will need more, and less costly, capital to take advantage of growing investment opportunities as well as to ward off increasingly competitive investors from around the world, who are often willing to accept lower rates of return than we are accustomed to. But a higher rate of savings in itself will not solve our economic dilemma in coming years.[31]

=

It is also widely claimed that a shortage of skills among American workers limits economic growth, especially as new computerized technologies requiring more sophisticated workers become commonplace. Higher educational standards, according to this argument, will in themselves improve our economy significantly. But if anything, this may put the cart before the horse. It was rapid economic growth and rising opportunity that provided the main incentive, as well as the funds, for improving the quality and broadening the availability of education over our history. Americans first developed their new public schools in the mid-nineteenth century to prepare their children for the booming commercial economy. The same was true for the expansion of the high school system beginning at the turn of the century, and for colleges and universities when returning veterans took advantage of the GI Bill in huge numbers after World War II. Americans generally went to school to get ahead, and the great innovation of the American education system was that it served this vocational purpose by providing the basic skills for holding jobs and rising in a commercial society.[32] Even our higher education was essentially geared not to the traditional classical standards that once included Greek and Latin, but to practical pursuits such as agriculture, engineering, law, medicine, and business administration.[33]

But in the past twenty years, contrary to conventional wisdom, we have not created enough of the kinds of jobs that make a basic education pay off the way it once did, especially as the costs of education have risen rapidly. When wages for high school graduates began to fall sharply, adjusted for inflation, in the early 1970s, the perceived value of a high school diploma fell with them. Sloughing off and dropping out began to make better sense to many youngsters, especially at lower economic levels. For a while in the 1970s the prospects for college graduates, who make up about 25 percent of the workforce, also declined sharply, which probably also further discouraged high school students from taking their education as seriously as they once did. The economy simply could not absorb the large numbers of college-educated baby boomers entering the job market in the 1970s. As economist Richard Freeman concludes in his book *The Overeducated American,* the rate of return on a college education, based on the salaries the graduates were getting, fell to postwar lows in these years.[34] College enrollments fell in the 1970s as a result. Thus, in a period of stagnant or declining real wages, the profitability of education also declines, and many students, parents, and even communities reduce the priority they once gave education. The investment in education by the United States fell from 4.7 percent of the economy between 1959 and 1971 to 2.7 percent between 1971 and 1985. The quality of our education has faltered as a result, and crime and drugs have become increasingly enticing alternatives for the young.[35]

In the 1980s the relative payoff for going to college began to rise again, and indeed a higher proportion of high school students began to enroll in two-year and four-year colleges. However, this occurred not because salaries for college graduates rose rapidly but because opportunities for those with four years of high school or less continued to fall sharply. Even though the average pay for a college graduate rose by only 3 percent in total between 1979 and 1989, this nevertheless represented a salary that by the end of the decade was 70 percent higher than what the average high school graduate was earning.[36] A college education did not assure an American youngster a standard of living that would rise as rapidly as it did in the 1950s and 1960s, but a high school diploma no longer assured youngsters a decent chance to remain in the middle class at all.

If technology had changed so rapidly since 1980 that skilled college graduates were in serious short supply, as some maintain, their salaries would probably have risen much more than they did throughout the 1980s. But there has been evidence of only local and temporary shortages of workers. By 1987, as we noted in the last chapter, average salaries for workers with college degrees also started to fall, and kept falling even during the economic expansion of the 1990s.[37] The average hourly wage of a worker with a four-year college degree dropped from $15.98 in 1987 to $15.71 in 1993.[38] And new research showed that the incomes earned by workers with similar college educations were also highly unequal.[39] To some degree, college graduates were being hired for jobs that once went to high school graduates, which lowered their earnings and made matters even worse for less-educated workers.[40] International competition was adding to the pressure on the earnings of skilled workers as the educational level of workforces even in developing countries was rising.[41] Ironically, the pay gap between better-educated and less-educated workers may narrow in coming years now that more high school graduates are enrolling in higher education. This could discourage students once again from going to college.

History suggests that the best cure for our educational system is a thriving economy in which business creates jobs that provide a substantial payoff for learning and investing in specialized job training. But if growth remains slow, improving educational quality will remain elusive. There is no evidence for the disturbing claim that many American workers lack the innate ability to keep up with technological change. Though some have been deprived of educational possibilities because of the deterioration of inner cities or the rising costs of higher education compared with shrinking and stagnant wages, there has been no serious unmet demand for skilled workers in the American economy to date. If demand for talent rises, the American worker will probably respond to opportunity as quickly as he or she always has, as long as the costs of education are affordable and proportionate to the rewards. If slow economic growth persists, meeting these two conditions will be difficult.

The need for a more highly skilled workforce will probably grow in coming years as businesses reform and modernize around the world. But deteriorating educational standards in America are so far more a consequence of slow economic growth than a cause of it. The quality of American education always made its greatest strides in times of rapid economic growth. We have never before faced the problem of raising the educational standard of the population dramatically in a time of entrenched slow growth.[42]

=

Many economists and businessmen also look forward to the economic development of emerging nations as a source of new markets and growth for us. This view is no doubt colored by the rapid growth of markets for our goods in Europe and Japan after World War II. On balance, economic development around the world will continue to benefit us for the same reasons that free trade in general has. We all grow faster by selling more of the goods that each of us makes most expertly and efficiently; in other words, we all gain from one another's specialization, including our own. Reduced barriers to trade have thus enhanced the economic growth of the members of the Common Market. This thinking motivated the adoption of the North American Free Trade Agreement, which reduces trade barriers between the United States, Mexico, and Canada.

But the development of these new markets is not an unalloyed good, either, because emerging nations, especially now, tend to grow most quickly by making the goods richer nations need—in other words, by competing with us. The rapidly developing countries on the Pacific Rim, including Japan, Korea, Malaysia, Taiwan, Singapore, and Hong Kong, have generally stimulated growth by cultivating industries that specialize in exports. Soon they also made many of the products their own consumers demanded. Since the 1980s, we have spent about $100 billion more on goods each year from these countries than we have sold to them.[43] Our trade deficit with China alone, negligible through most of the 1980s, came to $29.5 billion in 1994. Ultimately, even our trade surplus with South America, the only region in the world where we have such a surplus, will probably narrow as these nations begin to develop more sophisticated economies. Moreover, if the surplus doesn't narrow, political pressure will ultimately restrict American exports to these countries.

Unrestricted foreign competition can also retard the development of new industries and the revitalization of old valuable ones at home as cheaper imports discourage such industries in advanced nations from entering the market.[44] Rapid growth in emerging economies also penalizes advanced nations by attracting capital in search of higher profits. In 1994 America sent $14.4 billion more in equity capital to other nations than it received, compared with only $8.5 billion in 1990.[45] While the outflow of capital is still relatively small, we should remember that the decline of the economies that had successively led the world since the Middle Ages— the Italian city-states, Holland, and then Britain—were all accompanied by aggressive investment in business overseas rather than at home.

Many newly developing nations, especially those with stable authoritarian governments, will also maintain their competitive advantages in low wages and other costs of production far longer than Japan or Western Europe were able to do. For example, even if China grows as fast in the next ten years as it has in the past ten, its average wage will rise from 1.9 percent to only 3.2 percent of ours.[46] Some of these nations will enter the already crowded market for high-technology products as well. On balance, as we have said, free trade and worldwide economic development will help us. But there is no windfall for America any longer in the development of markets overseas as there was immediately after World War II, when we more or less monopolized worldwide production.

=

To accept the possibility that there may be no overall solution to our slow economic growth is painful to Americans, which is probably why we find so little discussion of such gloomy prospects in the media or even on university campuses, to say nothing of what politicians tell us. We embrace solutions like those offered above with enthusiasm, trusting that once they are adopted everything will be all right again. Bad news goes against the grain of our traditional optimism. Rival politicians denounce incumbents and feel bound to offer a vision of the future as rosy as the past if only their own policy recommendations are adopted, recommendations that now usually include lower taxes, less expensive government, and a return to the romanticized virtues of our past, such as stable families, adherence to religion, and personal responsibility. Economic experts are also given to optimistic diagnoses that produce the sorts of recommendations we have discussed above. One television producer I know insisted that his nightly broadcasts always include solutions to whatever problems may have been raised, thereby strictly limiting, wittingly or not, the kinds of problems suitable for discussion. Like nearly everyone else, he was bowing to America's optimism.

Optimism served us well as our economy grew, but it also mutes self-criticism and narrows our perspective in precarious times. Our optimism originated, as we have seen, in our colonial experience, when unprecedented opportunity and growing wealth justified the self-confident outlook that led to the American Revolution, and it became increasingly ingrained in us beginning early in the 1800s, when the pace of economic growth quickened rapidly. Average Americans remained anxious about their prospects, of course, but economic growth, spreading opportunity at home and on the frontier, and rising wages gradually emboldened them. The new evangelical movements that more or less began in the 1820s and came to be known as the Second Great Awakening, for example, promised that simple faith (and a conversion) was the road to salvation. If you believed you could be saved, and led a life of self-restraint, you would be saved. You might even enjoy some more material benefits along the way. Under the old Calvinist religion only a select few could be saved, but under these new theologies everyone could be saved.[47]

Antislavery, temperance, and women's movements, which arose in these same years, were also grounded in this rising optimism, assuring their followers a better life if only they followed their particular creeds. The various faiths were borne out by rapid economic growth. Manifest Destiny, the Indian Wars, and abolitionism were all ignited by this optimism about American possibilities—that, respectively, we could tame the frontier, subdue "barbaric" civilizations, and demonstrate that all men were created equal.

Optimism coexisted with a strain of pessimism throughout our history. John Adams's Federalists feared unbridled democracy. Many of the evangelical movements of the Second Great Awakening, like many of the social reform movements, were initially an angry response to the proliferation of worldly goods.[48] True believers endured earthly sacrifice, expecting salvation to arrive only with the millennium. In these evangelical movements were the seeds of the conspiratorial paranoia that culminated in the extreme populism of the 1890s, the McCarthyism of the 1950s, and some "radical right" movements today.

But rapid economic growth generally subdued the more extreme elements, and optimism prevailed. This optimism about America, sustained by widening prosperity, inspired political leaders from Jackson and Lincoln to Franklin D. Roosevelt, whose assurance during the Great Depression that we had nothing to fear but fear itself was every bit as ingenuously optimistic as was Herbert Hoover's less eloquent insistence that all the nation lacked was confidence in itself.[49]

In our time, Richard Nixon's vice president Spiro Agnew denounced the "nattering nabobs of negativism," and Ronald Reagan told us that "It's morning again in America." Reagan called his critics pessimists, and pessimism he believed was un-American. "Our optimism has once again been turned loose," he declared in his 1980 campaign. "And all of us recognize that these people who keep talking about the age of limits are really talking about their own limitations, not America's."[50] During the 1992 presidential campaign, President Bush also called his political enemies pessimists when they suggested that the economy was not recovering as quickly as he insisted it was. Ross Perot at least confronted America's slow growth when he ran for president in 1992. But the source of his popularity was his optimistic promise that cutting the federal deficit was the certain and obvious way out of our problems. In a commencement speech at UCLA in 1994, Bill Clinton continued this American refrain, warning the graduating class away from its pessimism and "a sense of generational despair that our glory days are behind us."[51]

An unintended consequence of such "positive" thinking is to make us angrily blame one another for our problems. The belief that somebody must be taking advantage of us rather than that something might be wrong—or different—with the American economy is a typical reaction to our confusion. It is easier to blame big government, big business, foreign competitors, minorities, immigrants, welfare recipients, criminals, labor unions, a liberal conspiracy, or extramarital sex on the part of our politicians than to confront the reality of declining growth and the hard choices that it implies. If we just cure a few of these defects, we presume we can return to that heroic period when our economy grew rapidly. The search for something or somebody to blame is not limited to political conservatives. "It's not that the nation has gotten poorer. It hasn't," writes a liberal commentator, Mickey Kaus, "but money is increasingly something that enables the rich, and even the merely prosperous, to live a life apart from the poor."[52] But, as we have seen, economic prospects have become manifestly worse for the large majority of us, and this has nothing to do with whether or not the rich live apart from the poor.

Time and again, we have been told by experts and politicians that we are back on track, especially when the Republicans were in power during the economic expansion of the 1980s. That temporary prosperity was fueled by an unparalleled growth in federal debt from about $1 trillion to more than $4 trillion. The underlying economy, in fact, remained weak during the Republican decade. Productivity grew at only 1 percent a year, and wages fell for many workers. In the mid-1990s, we are also told—now by the Democrats in power as well—that the economy is climbing out of its morass, and that our productivity problems are being solved. Yet, as of the end of 1994, the economic expansion that began in 1991 produced no real wage gains and no faster growth in productivity than other expansions of the past two decades, despite record levels of worker layoffs. Unsurprisingly, a broad voter survey before the 1994 election found that the electorate was still "angry, self-absorbed and politically unanchored."[53]

Pessimists have usually been wrong about America, and for good reason. Ralph Waldo Emerson's optimistic individualism was more farsighted than the later pessimism of such writers as Frederick Jackson Turner and Henry Adams. Man could do anything, especially American man. He could conquer nature and space. "Let man, then, learn," wrote Emerson in his famous 1847 essay "Self-Reliance," "that the Highest dwells with him."[54] A half century later, the great American philosopher William James warned against optimists who think "salvation is inevitable."[55] With luck, the "world may be saved," he said, but generations will come and go as they always have. We may yet, in our straitened circumstances, remake our lives on a sounder basis than in the past, becoming less dependent on material gain. We may yet be able to manage well in the new world economy, as individuals and as a nation. But we will not do so by optimistically assuming that this new world has remained as accommodating as its predecessor and all that ails us is that we have taken a wrong moral or ideological turn.

Chapter 5

LOST
BEARINGS

Unlike the dramatic consequences of a market crash or a sudden steep recession, the damage done by slow economic growth, as I said at the beginning of this book, accumulates gradually and mostly imperceptibly. This is why it becomes increasingly disorienting to us. Both individually and as a nation, we know from our own experience that we are less well-off, but we don't know why or by how much, or whether the damage is permanent or merely temporary, the result of a serious shift in our collective fortunes or of a passing disturbance. The bitter public debate over a national health-care bill in the summer of 1994 is a good example of this confusion. The difficulty in finding common ground for comprehensive health-care reform, once so widely favored, was blamed on well-financed special interests, a weak president, rising concerns over big government, and the complexity of the legislation itself. But the underlying problem was slow economic growth.

Had the economy grown as rapidly since the early 1970s as it had over the preceding century, rising health-care expenditures would have come to only 11 percent to 12 percent of GDP by the early 1990s, not the 14 percent of GDP that we find unmanageable. Most of us would have been able to buy enough medical coverage on our own if we so chose, and far fewer people would have had to go without insurance at all. For the government to fill the remaining gaps in coverage would have required a new federal program less ambitious than the ones that were proposed, and we also would have had much more tax revenue with which to pay for it. Pinched for two decades by stagnating incomes, Americans were not about to open their purses for a costly new social program or to tolerate a wider federal budget deficit. Forced to come up with a health-care package that did not require significant new taxes, the president and Congress devised proposals that in turn demanded sacrifices by too many groups, including reduced services and fewer choices for the people already insured.[1]

In the past we did not as a rule wonder where the money would come from to pay for our social programs. If we hesitated to adopt these programs, the reason was more a consequence of our historic preference for minimal government than that we couldn't afford them. No broad political consensus opposed massive pensions paid to Civil War veterans in the 1870s or Social Security or unemployment insurance in the 1930s.[2] Social Security and unemployment insurance expenditures soared after World War II as benefits were extended with comparatively little thought of their cost. We adopted Medicare in 1965, remarkably enough, without restricting the costs of the services the federal government was willing to reimburse. We mistakenly believed Lyndon Johnson's claim that we could fight the Vietnam war and finance the Great Society at the same time without raising taxes. And why not? Economic growth had always exempted us from serious personal sacrifices as we paid for the social and other domestic programs we agreed were necessary.[3] By the time of the health-care debate in 1994 this was obviously no longer true.

=

Americans have generally underestimated how unusual our economic advantages once were, how they have shaped us individually, and how they have influenced the way we solve our social problems. The economic progress most Americans have enjoyed since the early 1800s, and which we still take largely for granted, was unprecedented. Economic data were not gathered systematically in the nineteenth century, but from what historians have learned from local histories, personal diaries, the financial accounts kept by stores and other businesses, and the examination of wage records of such institutions as the army and the Erie Canal, a general picture clearly emerges of a rising standard of living in both rural and urban America. Beginning in the 1830s, Americans were rapidly replacing their one- and two-room cottages with the balloon-frame two-story houses that became the new standard. Over the years, we were increasingly able to buy good stoves, candle lamps for reading, hardware for doors and windows, and pillows, mattresses, and sheets to replace the straw mats and blankets we once slept on. Rural families bought more reliable wagons, and city families bought factory-made clothes for men. With their extra money, Americans bought almanacs, newspapers, and schoolbooks for their children. The more people spent, the more our economy grew. Our prosperity was self-reinforcing as our insatiable markets for goods of all kinds expanded.[4]

In the mid-nineteenth century the sewing machine had become almost as obligatory in American households as TV sets were in the 1950s, and many if not most people soon owned a few kerosene lamps, creating a petroleum boom a generation before automobiles arrived.[5] Children typically went to school because Americans could at last afford not to have them work at home, on the farm, or in factories. By then the American public grade school system was already envied around the world.[6] In those years the belief in the "self-made man" became a national orthodoxy, justified not so much by the number of people who struck it rich but by the general rise in real incomes for most Americans.[7] After the Civil War rising real wages enabled Americans to buy up the new mass-produced clocks, firearms, light mobile wagons and carriages, bicycles, packaged and processed foods, soap, cigarettes, and, of course, land that represented an improving standard of living.

In the twentieth century incomes grew still faster. In the Roaring Twenties, as we have noted, the economy grew at a rate of 6 percent a year and productivity at 4 percent a year. By 1930, 60 percent of American families owned some 25 million cars. Only a relative handful had owned cars twenty years earlier. Seventeen million American families owned their homes. Many of these homes had electricity, washing machines, refrigerators, phonographs, and plumbing.[8] Radios transformed the nation in the 1930s, as half of us got our news over the new talking box rather than from newspapers.[9] The new "talkies" of the late 1920s evolved in only a few years to become the sophisticated movies of Hollywood's golden years. Hollywood became a mass-market industry only because so many Americans had the time and the money to go to the movies, even during the Great Depression. Over these years, Americans felt rich enough to make school attendance mandatory. By 1930 a majority of teenagers were attending high school.[10]

As early as the 1820s, the term "middle class" was used to describe those Americans who had risen above the common standard of the Old World.[11] But expectations rise quickly, and only after World War II did the majority of Americans earn what we now consider the minimum entitlements of the middle class. In the 1940s fewer than half of all American families owned their own homes, a refrigerator, or a vacuum cleaner. The same proportion of American families as in the late 1920s, only three out of five, owned a car. One out of three homes had no running water, two out of five had no flush toilets, and most of the homes were not centrally heated. Living conditions were crowded, compared with what we are used to today. More than two out of three unmarried adults lived with their parents, and about one out of four elderly lived with their children.[12] According to one poll, only 37 percent of Americans in the early 1950s thought of themselves as middle-class.[13]

But as family incomes doubled from about $18,100 to $36,900 between 1947 and 1973 (measured in 1993 dollars), the broad middle-class majority was created.[14] By 1970 four out of five American families owned at least one car, two out of three had a washing machine, and almost all families had a refrigerator. About 65 percent of American families owned their own homes, and almost all had flush toilets and running water.[15] The proportion of white males who had graduated from college rose from 6 percent in 1947 to 11 percent in 1959 and to about 25 percent in the 1980s.[16] More than half of working Americans had a private pension, compared with only about 15 percent after World War II, supplementing Social Security benefits, which themselves were only a generation old.[17]

Financial progress, though volatile, became increasingly reliable over the course of our history and was the central determining factor in our history. In America, poor youngsters could occasionally rise to wealth, the manual worker to a desk job, the farmer's son to the big-city law firm. John Jacob Astor began as a butcher and became a multimillionaire as well as a leader of New York society. By the time he died in 1848 there were some sixty millionaires in America when room and board in New York's best hotel cost no more than $1.20 a day. Benjamin Franklin's rags-to-riches autobiography became a best-seller early in the nineteenth century and was followed by a long list of imitators, culminating in the Horatio Alger stories. But this, of course, was not the typical experience. Our social mobility was widespread rather than dramatic. Though incomes were volatile, most Americans made more money over time, bought the new consumer goods, and had more leisure, whether or not they climbed more than a rung or two on the social ladder. A large and growing number of Americans could buy a house, and through a long-standing job or the ownership of a business, and by accumulating savings, could increasingly guarantee themselves a secure old age and give their children a financial start.[18] The generation that followed expected to make still more, and these expectations were usually met and exceeded.

Over most of these years life was harsh by modern standards. Along with widespread prosperity, the incidence of poverty also rose and recessions were often severe. Many lived in squalor. Some ethnic groups did more poorly than others. But economic progress became comparatively steady for most Americans, especially by Old World standards. Average real wages, though they often fell over short periods of time, rose over every ten-year period in both the nineteenth and twentieth centuries, with the exception of the Civil War and the years that followed. Unemployment also rose in the nineteenth century, but to levels only slightly higher than they are today, and, as noted, the duration of unemployment was typically shorter.[19] By 1900 the average real income was about three times what it had been in 1800, and by 1990 the average American was spending approximately four times what Americans had spent on consumer goods in 1900.[20]

The ability to buy more goods and real property was the source of our personal self-esteem from the very beginning, enabling Americans to disregard Old World class structures and abandon the assumptions that birthright determined status and scarcity was a fact of life. This breadth of material opportunity was liberalizing and even radicalizing, and inspired the unprecedented, even startling idea that equality of opportunity was a desirable and some thought an attainable good. The excitement of gaining some measure of financial security, material comfort, and self-esteem—Frederick Jackson Turner's "competency"—for a people whose Old World ancestors never expected such advantages vitalized the nation. As early as the eighteenth century, many colonial Americans openly displayed the material possessions that announced their newfound economic status. By the 1790s average Americans were eschewing with relish knee breeches and old titles such as "esquire" that represented the hierarchical style of the Old World. By the early 1800s Catherine Sedgwick, a descendant of one of the Federalist families, concluded: "Wealth, you know, is the grand leveling principle."[21] These values were reinforced over time. Honest effort, aggressiveness, self-reliance, optimism—all these American characteristics brought both substantially more material reward and personal security than was expected as the century progressed, reinforcing our idea that working hard was a sign of one's moral worth and the acquisition of material goods the outward proof of it. More Americans making more money was, in fact, the true American experience. Such ascendancy was perhaps as exciting to those who reached the middle class after World War II as it had been to the first Americans who escaped the chains of the Old World. Steady financial progress for most of us was part and parcel of American life and the foundation of our national character.

=

By the early 1970s, as we have seen, this rapid progress had slowed sharply for the large majority of Americans, and was reversed for many of us. Economic growth, which, as we know, had averaged more than 3.5 percent a year since 1820, had fallen to a rate of 2.3 percent a year since 1973. The average wage of the 80 percent of American workers who were nonmanagerial also fell over this twenty-year period, probably the longest such decline since the industrial revolution began, with the possible exception of the years after the Civil War. Average wages fell consistently even during the long debt-fueled expansion of the 1980s.[22] The average American family earned only about $1,500 more than the average family did in 1973, income rising from $36,900 to $38,400, only because so many spouses went to work.[23] The standard of living by and large fell, stagnated, or grew very slowly for most Americans, even though we were working longer and harder.

Signs of the uneasiness and confusion resulting from slow economic growth are all around us, perhaps most clearly in the extent to which Americans have lost faith in traditional institutions. Two decades ago about 42 percent of Americans reported that they had "a lot of confidence" in Congress. In the summer of 1994 only 18 percent had as much confidence. A decline of faith in Congress may not be surprising, but, over the same two decades, confidence in public schools and banks dropped by 25 percent, in TV news and newspapers by about 20 points, and in organized religion and the Supreme Court by 10 points. Overall, two out of three Americans reported in a 1994 survey that they believed the nation was heading in the wrong direction, a surprise perhaps to those who believed the economic expansion of the 1990s would relieve some of these concerns.[24]

Increasingly insecure about our place in society and among our families, friends, and communities, and finding that working harder and longer doesn't make us better off, we have become understandably nostalgic for an era of fast economic growth when families seemed to be financially secure, government did not encumber our standard of living, and our financial expectations were usually met and often surpassed. As our old values have become increasingly undependable, many Americans have looked elsewhere for stable ground: personal fitness, psychotherapies of many kinds, exotic religions and new orthodoxies, new strains of feminism, environmentalism, and, of course, "family values." The increasing popularity of third-party and independent political candidates is typical of this struggle to find answers to the unprecedented shift in our fortunes. The surprising success of Ross Perot's presidential campaign in 1992 was only one example of this tendency. The number of third-party and independent candidates doubled between 1986 and 1994. In a preelection survey in the fall of 1994, 53 percent of the respondents believed there should be a third political party in America.[25] In the 1994 elections the electorate savaged incumbents from coast to coast, often in search of "old values." Yet, to the extent that the "values" voters were searching for ever actually existed, they reflected the dependably growing prosperity of earlier times and not the superior moral attributes of an earlier generation of politicians.

This frustration also accounts for our rising anger and divisiveness. Since at least the early 1980s, critics have called attention to a new separatism among ethnic and religious groups that extends from the suburbs and ghettos to high schools and college campuses. The degree of separatism has only increased. In 1994 suburban communities in Washington, Dallas, and elsewhere tried to ban churches that provide services to the poor, new immigrants, or other unwelcome groups.[26] In Alabama a high school principal forbade interracial dating at the senior prom, and throughout the United States, African-American college students, denouncing integration in favor of empowerment, increasingly separated themselves from the rest of the student body.[27] In the suburbs, segregation became a way of life. Ninety-five percent of blacks on Long Island, New York, for example, lived in only 5 percent of the census tracts.[28] In a Florida county a religious organization demanded that schoolchildren be taught that American values are superior to all others, a reaction to the demands of various American ethnic groups for inclusion of their respective heritages in our public school curricula.[29] The state of California voted to deny public services to illegal immigrants, including school for their children. Between Washington and local lawmakers, partisan animosity rose, as they found it increasingly difficult to satisfy their unhappy constituents by providing them with new programs. Political pundits blamed this on politics as usual; more likely, it was the result of slow growth. As we have seen, Congress was almost unable to pass the widely popular but stripped-down crime bill in the summer of 1994 largely because there was not enough pork to pass around to the warring constituencies. The new Speaker of the House, Newt Gingrich, suggested putting children of impoverished parents in orphanages and refusing benefits to unwed mothers, a trivial contribution at best to our fiscal balance, but attractive to many frightened and angry voters.

Americans have often been in conflict before, of course. Today's public anxiety over national values and our common future recalls the unrest of the early 1800s as the United States was transforming itself from a traditional agrarian economy to a largely mercantile and industrial one that lifted incomes quickly and broadly. Strains brought about by this new commercial economy—emigration from farms to increasingly dense cities and the widespread creation of new wealth, which challenged the traditional agricultural hierarchy—produced a contentious social, political, and religious environment in which, as we have seen, the old Calvinism gave way to the democratic Christianity of the Second Great Awakening, in which anyone, not just a chosen elite, could be saved. From this same democratic fervor arose feminism and abolitionism, labor unions, and temperance societies, as well as the political movements that eventually won universal suffrage for all white males, not simply men of property as provided in the Constitution.

These battles in behalf of greater opportunity were not easily won. The new movements, as well as the new churches, were often antagonistic toward one another. But the dislocations they caused were typical of the turmoil that usually accompanies rapid economic transformation, in this case the same rapid transformation that inspired our national optimism and the faith, soon broadcast around the world, that America was the land of opportunity for all. As we have seen, incomes periodically fell but typically rose again within a matter of years. As markets grew and productivity increased, the economy in general began to expand more rapidly. Material well-being and prosperity validated the principles of equality and democracy. The Emancipation Proclamation and the war that made it possible were rooted in the optimistic movements that emerged in the 1820s, culminating in Lincoln's claim that under God all men are created equal. (As for women, they would have to wait for the next century, although they were to win the right to vote in some western territories as early as the 1870s and 1880s.) Rapidly increasing prosperity ultimately fostered a national spirit of inclusion, tolerance, and compromise that enhanced the rights of the so-called common man as it would eventually those of blacks, new immigrants, and women, at least by the standards of the times, while it subdued the more pessimistic elements in our society. As we progressed materially we found common cultural and social ground to share. Prosperity was the foundation of our best convictions as a nation, for what equality of opportunity meant in a rising economy was that with a lot of hard work most Americans could live a decent life and expect better for their children.

The dislocations that we have experienced since the 1970s are also the results of an economic transformation, marked this time by narrowing opportunity over two long decades. As our material expectations are disappointed our new social, political, and religious movements become increasingly exclusionary, intolerant, and uncompromising, for now equality of opportunity implies sharing scarce resources, not voluntarily but under the compulsion of the government and the labor markets. No wonder that politicians often invoke an imagined golden age of stable nuclear families, frontier individualism, and opportunity for all, free of government interference and high taxes. But if slow economic growth stimulates such compensating illusions, it also destroys them as one set of political promises after another is inevitably broken, leaving many of us increasingly bitter and anguished as we grope for solutions that can't be found. This bitterness is likely to continue. Without increasing prosperity, Americans are losing the courage of the convictions they once shared. The idea of equality and the democratic values that accompany it are no longer as honored as they were when we were getting richer and could imagine prosperity for all. As personal resources decline and national prospects dim, we are losing our nerve as individuals. National paranoia shows signs of revival. We seek scapegoats and hide in illusions about our past. As many of us retreat to the safety of this imaginary past, we forget that the very forebears whom we invoke abandoned the exclusionary politics and social institutions of their own past as their economic environment improved.

=

The consequences of slow economic growth since 1973 have been borne more heavily by some of us than by others, but they have frustrated almost all of us in ways more or less subtle. Wages and salaries have fallen, stagnated, or grown unusually slowly for most Americans over these years, however well educated they were. Annual income has mostly stagnated even for the age group whose incomes typically rise fastest, twenty-five- to thirty-five-year-olds. The annual real income of the average twenty-five-year-old who went to work in the mid-1970s rose by only 16 percent by the time he or she was thirty-five. By contrast, the annual real income of the twenty-five-year-old worker who went to work in the 1950s or early 1960s doubled in just ten years.[30]

In part, it is inevitable that the losses have been especially steep for the young with only a high school education. These young and inexperienced workers are the first to lose their jobs when unemployment rises, as has happened consistently since the 1960s. But the jobs lost in manufacturing and other areas because of greater international competition, fragmenting markets, flexible production, and declining investment have taken a bigger toll on young and less educated workers as we recede from an economy dominated by mass production and distribution. Average real wages for workers between twenty-five and thirty-four with only a high school diploma fell by 12 percent in the eight years from 1979 to 1987, eight years that included the economic expansion of the 1980s that was celebrated for having produced so many new jobs. Twenty-five- to thirty-five-year-olds were earning a full 25 percent less after inflation in the early 1990s than twenty-five- to thirty-five-year-olds with the same experience were earning in the early 1970s.[31]

For minorities the picture is worse. From the 1960s to the 1970s, African Americans made rapid economic progress. The gap in pay between college-educated black and white Americans, for example, narrowed dramatically to a mere 3.7 percent in 1973. By 1989 that gap had opened to 15.5 percent. For black high school graduates, the gap widened from 10.3 percent in 1973 to 16.7 percent. A comprehensive study by econ-

omists Richard Freeman and John Bound found that the gap
between blacks and whites widened most in midwestern cities
mainly because of the loss of manufacturing jobs for black
workers. A slow-growth economy has amounted to a full-
fledged depression for these two groups, who have remained
near the bottom for the past twenty years.[32]

Severe damage done by the slow-growth economy has
spread beyond the young and those with only a high school
education, however. More people of all ages, no matter what
their ethnic group or educational qualifications, have lost jobs
than at any other time in the postwar era. The unemployment
rate alone does not tell the complete story. In 1990, for example, though the unemployment rate averaged 5.5 percent,
nearly 15 percent of all workers actually experienced a period
of unemployment during the year. The unemployed, both
blue- and white-collar, now remain out of work longer. Between 1973 and 1993, 40 percent to 50 percent of the unemployed were out of work for six months or longer, compared
with only 26 percent on average in the 1960s. Those who lost
jobs in the 1990s and found a new one took on average a pay
cut of 23 percent.[33]

As we have seen, the loss of middle-class production jobs in
manufacturing spearheaded this broad decline in economic
opportunity and social mobility. Good jobs in the other areas
of the economy that were related to mass production also
began to disappear or to pay less well. These included jobs in
giant distribution, retailing, and marketing companies, as well
as in the countless satellite companies that served the mass-

production and distribution giants. As slow growth persisted, the damage done eventually spread to all kinds of white-collar jobs, as salaries for better-educated workers began to fall. The number of professional and managerial jobs in manufacturing fell by more than 3 percent since 1988, for example. As we have seen, the average wage for college graduates has fallen since 1987. Nor did experience or seniority protect a white-collar job any longer. After the economic expansion was well under way in the 1990s, older, highly paid white-collar workers were being rehired far more slowly than they once were. The unemployment rate of the two million college-educated white males aged forty-five to fifty-four rose rapidly between 1988 and 1992 as their average earnings fell by 17 percent over these years.[34]

More than 40 percent of American workers in a 1991 survey reported that there were large layoffs in their companies. In the same survey, 28 percent of workers reported widespread layoffs among managers. Instability also affected those who owned their own businesses, often the satellite companies that supply our larger firms.[35] The rate of business failures rose by two and a half times between the 1970s and 1980s, from around 40 per ten thousand companies to more than 100, where it has more or less remained even during the expansion of the 1990s.[36] Economic insecurity has spread across working America, no matter one's ethnic origin or education.

Falling or stagnating wages for so many Americans have resulted in a gap between high and low wage earners that by the early 1990s was wider than at any time since the end of the Great Depression. The proportion of middle-income workers fell. Over these same years, the number of poor grew from about 11 percent of the total population to more than 15 percent, including a rapidly growing number who were working full-time and still earning only poverty-level wages. Their proportion rose by 50 percent since 1980 from 12 percent of the workforce to 18 percent in 1992. Of those under twenty-five with full-time jobs, the proportion who earned only a poverty-level income rose from 23 percent in 1980 to 47 percent in 1992.[37] The top 20 percent of the population was the only quintile whose share of total income rose in the 1980s, though even their incomes grew only modestly on average.[38] This group was made up largely of college graduates in such fields as sales, engineering, health care, finance, law, and administration, but its members often fell out of the quintile as they were replaced temporarily by others. Only a relatively small proportion of Americans, then, was making any significant, consistent financial progress in these years. By 1993, the lowest-paid 10 percent of workers in America earned 38 percent of average earnings of all workers. By contrast, the lowest-paid 10 percent of workers in Europe earned 68 percent of the average worker's pay. A joint study by the Labor and Commerce departments concluded in 1994 that the distribution of income in America "is the most unequal among developed countries," a startling departure from America's early days.[39] Yet even the gains made on average by those in the top 20 per-

cent were moderate compared with those made in the immediate post–World War II period.

=

Despite the presumption by some that too many Americans are not working hard enough, Americans in fact
responded to their changing economic fortunes by working
much harder. The average full-time male employee now
works about a week and a half longer a year than in 1973, the
first extended increase in hours worked in this century.[40]
Seven million workers hold at least two jobs, the highest proportion in fifty years.[41] The number of two-worker families
rose by more than 20 percent in the 1980s. Some spouses went
back to work because they wanted to, but surveys showed that
most went to work in order to supplement the family income;
the largest increase in the proportion of working spouses was
among the families that earned the least money.[42] Working
more hours has in itself amounted to a serious reduction in
the standard of living for a growing proportion of Americans.

But this increased effort did not offset the damage done by
slow growth. Though mortgage rates fell sharply between
1991 and 1993, the resulting rise in home buying was not
enough to change more than marginally a long-term pattern
of declining homeownership among those in the prime
home-buying years. Only 34.6 percent of those aged twenty-
five to twenty-nine owned a home in 1993 compared with 43.6
percent in 1973. Of those between the ages of thirty and

thirty-four, only 51.0 percent owned a home in 1993 compared with 60.2 percent in 1973 (see Figure 7 in the Appendix).[43] The proportion of foreclosures rose steadily from .27 percent of residential mortgages in the late 1970s to a high of 1.12 percent in 1987, and improved only to 1.04 percent by mid-1994.[44]

Meanwhile the number of autos purchased per worker has fallen fairly steadily since the 1970s, as the price of a new car rose faster than average incomes (see Figure 8 in the Appendix). The age of the typical family car reached its highest level since 1948, cars ten years old or more accounting for about 30 percent of all outstanding cars in 1992 compared with only about 10 percent in the early 1970s. This is only partly explained by the improved durability of cars.[45] Detroit increasingly aimed its products at more affluent Americans, relegating low-income workers to the used-car lot.[46]

Similarly, tuition, room, and board at private colleges rose from 23 percent of the average family's income to 31 percent over these years. The cost of public colleges rose 50 percent faster than inflation over the past decade, though they were reducing the curricula and services they offered. Young people had to extend their college years while they worked to pay their tuition or because courses were unavailable. This took years from their careers. A growing proportion of them, some 13 percent in 1993 compared with 8 percent in the mid-1980s, relied for their tuition on their families.[47] The cost to a community to put a child through public school for a year has doubled since 1970, after inflation, while, as we know, incomes generally stagnated, resulting in widespread cutbacks in public-education budgets in rich as well as poor communities.[48]

Because of the loss of good jobs and changing corporate practices, only about 45 percent of all male workers participated in a private pension plan in 1992 compared with about 54 percent in the late 1970s. For workers between twenty-five and thirty-four with twelve years or less of schooling, the proportion of those covered by a pension plan fell from 49 percent to 23 percent.[49] Also, according to the Congressional Budget Office, most new pension plans no longer guarantee a defined benefit on retirement but only contribute a sum of money each year to an employee's retirement account, requiring workers to manage their own investments for better or worse.[50] Because of reduced coverage as well as slower-growing incomes in general, one consulting firm projects that most baby boomers now in their thirties and early forties will have only 50 percent to 60 percent of the income they will need, even if they own their own homes, for the comfortable retirement they still seem to expect. For those who don't own homes, their retirement income will most likely come to only 20 percent or 30 percent of what they need.[51]

Corporations are also rescinding medical benefits for retirees, eliminating them for future retirees, and reducing and sometimes eliminating coverage for current employees. The proportion of workers who receive health benefits from their employers fell from 67 percent in 1988 to 61 percent in 1993. Many health plans have also become more restrictive, often requiring contributions from workers.[52] Small companies in general have been unable to afford the rising costs of employee health insurance. In general, America is evolving into a two-tier society, and the upper tier is gradually shrinking.

An aging population will keep the pressure on cost cutting. By the next century the ratio of workers to the elderly will be 2 to 1 compared with 3.2 workers per elderly person today, making it more burdensome for future taxpayers to finance the Social Security system even if the economy resumes its historical rate of growth. If there were as few workers per retired person today as there will be a generation from now, the federal government would currently collect $220 billion a year less in taxes. To keep the Social Security system solvent in the next century could require an increase of as much as 3 to 5 percent more than today's regressive Social Security taxes of 12.4 percent of the first $61,200 of annual wages (half paid by the worker, half by the employer).[53] As baby boomers pass their fortieth birthday, there will be added pressure on health costs, probably no matter how we restrict the frequency of medical use and limit the costs of high-technology medicine. The Medicare system, for example, could well run out of money by the turn of the century. The alternative, of course, is to cut benefits, which is to say that a political confrontation between young taxpayers and elderly pensioners and Medicare and Medicaid recipients seems likely over the next two decades. The 1994 health-care debate anticipated this, as young healthy Americans revealed their reluctance to finance the growing health-care needs of the aging population.

=

Some experts argue that the quality, variety, and ingenuity of the new products of the past two decades have made up for our stagnating or falling wages and lost leisure time.[54] These experts say among other things that automobiles last longer, subways are air-conditioned, hundreds of thousands of people have been able to travel for low fares to vacations around the world, microwave ovens reduce the time we spend in the kitchen, homes are bigger, and medical care is better per dollar of expenditure than it was two decades ago. There are faxes, mobile phones, photocopiers, affordable stylish clothes. VCRs have made it much cheaper for the whole family to see a movie. Local cash machines mean that you no longer have to wait in line or rush to the bank by 3:00 P.M. Some economists say that because of all this we have underestimated the real productivity gains created by some new products and, especially, new services.

But "miraculous" new time-saving products have been coming along since the beginning of human culture. Man has always been making more and better tools. With the start of the industrial revolution, the pace of innovation accelerated rapidly. The reaper and thresher improved productivity and eliminated the worst kind of backbreaking farmwork, giving farmers free time at the end of the day. The kerosene lamp allowed average families to extend their activities economically well into the night, not to mention the benefits to stores, restaurants, and other public places. Imagine how the proliferation of affordable home sewing machines beginning in the mid-nineteenth century radically changed lifestyles and made housewives more "productive," or how the ability to buy cheap frozen meat at the corner grocer improved the family dinner with no additional and probably less effort. Or how the department store reduced the time required to shop. In 1843 it took forty days to cross the Atlantic from Liverpool to New York by sail. Thirty years later a steamer took only nine days, and eventually less than a week. In America the railroads reduced the cross-country trip from weeks to a few days. By the second half of the nineteenth century, cheap wagons and mass-produced bicycles also raised individual convenience and productivity dramatically, and eventually so did telephones and electricity. Almost overnight, Americans were spending their evenings in droves at the silent movies, and only a decade later at the talkies. Free TV in the 1950s probably seemed like a greater boon than the variety of choices on cable TV does today.

Not only have our new products always made our lives more comfortable, enjoyable, and productive, but more Americans could afford to buy them, and win status and economic security as well. We certainly have many remarkable new conveniences today, but it would be difficult to prove that they have improved our lives in greater increments than the products and services of the past.[55] The difference, however, is that now fewer and fewer Americans can afford to buy more and more, or have the financial peace of mind with which to enjoy them. New products have always provided greater convenience for Americans and made possible greater personal productivity. But these new products are not a substitute for spreading prosperity, growing incomes, rising homeownership, expanding leisure time, increasing access to a good education, more secure retirements, the steady climb toward the middle class by more and more Americans, and an economy whose bounty has consistently exceeded expectations—all of which characterized our history until 1973.

=

Education, hard work, good citizenship, voting and politicking, organized religion, and optimism are institutions and values worth defending in all circumstances. But they no longer guarantee us prosperity. No matter how hard we try, most of us make less money than we expected to, own less, don't know whether we can pay our medical expenses, and often can't buy a house. We worry more about our futures, whether we are just starting out or facing retirement. Even the suburbs are no longer a haven of prosperity. The average real income in more than one third of them declined between 1979 and 1989.[56]

Slow growth tests these fundamental values and the culture that embodies them. Given our traditional belief that financial failure reflects personal inadequacy, our collective and individual self-esteem, as well as our courage and identity, are casualties in an age of persistent slow growth as much as is our charity toward others. As slow growth continues, our anxiety may worsen and our public discourse become even more driven by fear. The social rifts that have already appeared may widen as we face a future for which our history has not prepared us.

=====

Chapter 6

WHAT WE FACE

The genius of a successful society is to solve its problems in unanticipated ways. Energy and innovation typically arise from surprising places, more often from the bottom than from the top. Our problems are now too broad and complex, and our society and its commerce too intricate and mature, I think, for us to expect Washington, a think tank, a university professor, or one of our transient prophets to show the way. Certainly, I shall not attempt to do so in this book. The answers to how we will deal with new circumstances will instead have to come from all of us at every level, as they usually have, through trial and error, experimentation, and persistence.

But we will arrive at only the wrong answers until we recognize that the potential for economic growth has probably been significantly, perhaps permanently, reduced as a result of the historic shift that I have attempted to describe in this book. Only when we shed our misplaced optimism and the illusions it fosters can we begin to redirect our diverse energies and embrace honest and able leaders, and a workable American agenda, once again. So far we have done none of these things. Instead, we have largely denied that our recurrent problems reflect a serious, underlying cause. Such denial is common among people with a new disease. They convince themselves that by thinking positively, by insisting they are as strong as ever, and by doing what they have always done, the affliction will disappear. They fight their symptoms rather than recognize the true malady, not out of ignorance but from fear. Often this fear turns to anger directed against the wrong culprits, including the doctor who tells them what the symptoms really mean. This search for scapegoats is as true of our collective behavior as a nation as it is of us as individuals.

=

No one can say with certainty, of course, that our rapid rate of economic growth won't return. Business reforms, interactive communications, new industrial techniques, overseas markets, and our progress in cutting the federal deficit and interest rates may produce faster economic growth than they have so far. Still other, unanticipated solutions for our slow growth may yet emerge. While in my view these prospects are remote, readers can determine reasonably well for themselves whether or not we are returning to rapid eco-

nomic growth by tracking several key statistics that economists and other specialists follow, and that can easily be found
in *The Wall Street Journal* and the financial pages of major
newspapers. The most important of these are the quarterly
productivity figures issued by the federal Bureau of Labor
Statistics. Because the growth rate of productivity differs
widely during various stages of the business cycle, a snapshot
of its current position will be misleading. To remain consistent with the historical norm, productivity growth should average about 2 percent a year over an entire business cycle,
from recovery and expansion through the next recession. In
the 1970s and 1980s, as we know, productivity generally
grew at an average of only about 1 percent a year over each
cycle.

The first of two important measures of worker compensation to consider is average weekly earnings, which measures
what 80 percent of American workers earn who are not in supervisory positions. The second measure is the employment
cost index, which includes all workers' wages, salaries, and
benefits, whether or not they are in management.[1] Both are re-
leased monthly by the Department of Labor. Readers should
also periodically check the growth of consumer borrowing
and the savings rate. The rate at which consumer installment
borrowing grows, which includes all credit-card debt and
auto loans, is published monthly by the Federal Reserve. The
savings rate is published monthly by the Department of
Commerce along with data on personal income and spending.

If borrowing remains historically high and the savings rate low, chances are that the underlying strength of an economic expansion is weaker than it may otherwise appear.

Though the economy grew at a rate of 4 percent in 1994, the cyclical recovery and expansion that began in 1991 showed no significant signs as of late that year of having overcome the slow growth of the preceding two decades. On average, as we noted, productivity grew no faster than it had during economic recoveries and expansions of the same duration in the 1970s and 1980s.[2] Average weekly wages actually fell slightly over the same period. The broader employment cost index showed a gain of only a few tenths of a percent a year after inflation.[3] In a historically normal economic expansion, these wages should have begun to rise by as much as 2 percent a year by the third year. The fall in weekly wages compared with the slight rise in the more comprehensive employee cost index, which includes supervisory and managerial workers, showed that the distribution of income had probably widened even more over these years. Meanwhile consumer borrowing grew at record rates by the end of 1994, and the savings rate remained historically low at about 4 percent to 5 percent of income.[4] These data suggested that 1994's pace of economic growth could not be sustained and that a serious slowdown, or perhaps even a recession, was likely within a year or two, well before either productivity or wages rose enough to support a higher level of economic growth.

=

If rapid economic growth returns, most of the acute social issues that worry us today will become manageable. Wages will rise, our Social Security, Medicare, and welfare commitments will be easily met, and we will generate enough resources to invest adequately in our future. Most Americans once again would make the kind of financial progress they had come to expect. But in the more likely case that historic growth is not restored, rising costs in both the private and public sectors, and growing demand for investment, will restrict our standard of living.

I don't have a blueprint for solving all the problems associated with slow growth. In any case, only when we see our problems for what they really are can we begin to fashion appropriate solutions. Nevertheless, the major issues that we must deal with forthrightly, and the key demands on our future resources, are fairly obvious. The unprecedented retirement and health costs associated with our aging population and the costs of a deteriorating environment will consistently require more of our future income. The interest on the debt consumers, business, and government assumed in the 1980s is another relatively new long-term cost that we did not have to bear in the past. Total household debt rose from 59 percent of annual income in 1973, for example, to 82 percent in 1993, and federal debt now amounts to about half of GDP, compared with less than a fifth in 1973.[5]

Meanwhile, with slow economic growth, it will cost taxpayers more to reduce or even contain poverty. Welfare programs may have inculcated a "dependency culture" among recipients, as social critics like Charles Murray have argued, but after twenty years of slow economic growth, and fewer and lower-paying jobs for less educated workers, it is also obviously harder to work one's way out of poverty, regardless of the presumed dependency.[6] The number of poor rose by nearly 7 million between 1989 and 1993, from 13 percent to 15 percent of the population. This can hardly have resulted simply from inadequate thirty-year-old welfare programs. In 1973, as noted, only 11 percent of the population was officially poor.[7] The number of those who work full-time and nevertheless earn a poverty-level wage has risen 50 percent since 1980, as we have seen, accounting for nearly one in five American workers. Estimates of those full-time workers who are "near-poor" have risen as fast.[8] The long-term consequences of this increased poverty are especially disturbing because indigence has fallen hardest on children, one out of five of whom, as we have noted, are now born into poverty-stricken homes.

We will also probably have to invest a greater proportion of our income, and to do so more deliberately than in the past. As we have seen in Chapter 4, decidedly more investment will be needed in research and development to maintain technological leadership, and new kinds of institutions to undertake the scientific research may have to be conceived, perhaps with help from public funds. Since 1985 our investment in R&D has not risen at all after discounting for inflation.[9]

Capital investment in traditional plant and equipment will probably require more of our resources if we are to stay competitive. A lack of capital wasn't a significant hindrance in the past two decades, in part because American business reformed slowly and had excess capacity. But as we have seen, flexible production, fragmenting markets, and aggressive world competitors will probably keep rates of return on investment both lower and more uncertain in the future than they have been in the past. Therefore, American business will have to put up more money, accept more risk, and invest for longer-term payoffs, perhaps again with help from public funds directly or through tax incentives. Though capital spending rose rapidly in 1993 and 1994, it grew no more quickly than it had during expansions of similar length in the 1970s and 1980s. And much of the capital spending has been for computerized equipment whose useful lives are unusually short and which will have to be upgraded or replaced frequently.[10]

Nor have we faced serious shortages of well-trained or well-educated workers over the past twenty years. But if we are to grow faster in the future, the average job will probably require a higher investment in education and job training than it once did, as production becomes more sophisticated. Many more jobs in corporate America involve the use of a computer.[11] Slow growth, however, has not only eroded the quality of our education as youngsters respond to an inadequate economic payoff, but the costs of education are also rapidly outpacing incomes for most Americans, making a standard education, from kindergarten to college, more costly to a growing segment of the American population. If we do not make a good education widely affordable, we may ultimately not only leave many Americans behind but fall short of enabling our business community to make the necessary reforms to compete successfully.

Rising wages, which give most Americans a stake in the future and a reason to work and invest in themselves, are essential to social harmony in modern times. When workers are in demand in a growing economy, ethnic or sexual prejudice diminishes, and labor unions find it easier to organize and win more benefits for their members. In times of rapid expansion, privilege typically plays a smaller role in determining who gets the better jobs, and more Americans can afford the education that will help them qualify for good jobs. When an economy grows slowly, the opposite occurs. Wages generally grow slowly or fall as labor becomes relatively abundant. The costs of education outpace slow-growing incomes. And the potential for abuse through prejudice, favoritism, and onerous management practices also rises. Because Americans have always believed that workers should be largely responsible for their own fortunes, neither our laws nor our customary business practices protect workers' wages and benefits the way they do in other countries.[12] Rapid economic growth enabled us to pay less attention to these matters than do other countries. All advanced nations today face much the same competitive pressures, yet American wage differentials, as we have seen, are much greater than they are elsewhere. The bottom tenth of our workers earns about half the salary that the bottom tenth of workers in Europe earns, and these nations have far fewer accidents at the workplace than we do as well.[13] Meanwhile, we don't make comparable investments in such areas as day care and job training that might help our workers become more productive.[14]

=

Although we are still the richest nation per capita in the world, we are not accustomed to making the kind of collective financial sacrifices appropriate to our newly reduced means. To this day, our tax rates are the lowest among advanced nations. Except for the post-Revolutionary period, Americans voluntarily accepted tax hikes that were large enough to reduce seriously the standard of living for a large proportion of them only during wartime: to pay the new income taxes to fight the Civil War, World War I, and World War II.[15] As we have seen, the social programs we have adopted since the Civil War have been paid largely from fast economic growth. Shared sacrifice is alien even to our labor unions, which have rarely agreed voluntarily to a reduced workweek for all their members in order to save jobs for everyone, as European unions often do.[16]

Instead of accepting shared sacrifice in times of need, we have become more vulnerable to fantasies of political escape offered up so liberally by politicians since the 1980s—the belief expressed in one form or other that all we have to do is behave "morally," "believe in ourselves," and get rid of bureaucracy in order to restore equity and social harmony. The Republican Contract with America implicitly promised that if we relied less on government and reduced our taxes, our deficits would vanish and prosperity would return. The Contract promised that we could afford a tax cut, raise military spending, guarantee future Social Security benefits, and balance the federal budget all at once. It is disheartening that after twenty years of slow growth Americans should accept such empty promises. Such nonsense reflects both the ambitions of cynical and timid politicians afraid to tell the truth and the wishful thinking of a fearful, angry electorate. We tested a similar approach in the 1980s, when we subscribed to the popular delusion that supply-side economics would solve the problem of slow growth. Three trillion dollars later, we saw that deep tax cuts, more military spending, and a reduced welfare state did not reinvigorate capital spending, productivity, or wages but, instead, created a mountain of public and private debt and enriched a fraction of a fraction of the population as millions of Americans descended into poverty.[17]

These are the fantasies of a nation that stubbornly denies its own vulnerability. The Contract with America and similar proposals depend less on serious economic analysis than on a cynical appeal to the moral themes of the Second Great Awakening when optimistic faith and economic miracles actually did go hand in hand, though it was economic growth that led and faith that followed, not the other way around. In a survey in the fall of 1994, nearly 60 percent of white Americans blamed our problems on deteriorating moral values.

Hardly anyone seemed to think that the slowing economy undermined our families, trashed our cities, or encouraged crime and a drug culture in the absence of lawful ways to make a reasonable living.[18] Today, more than 6 percent of America's working-age male population is either in prison or on parole or probation.[19]

It doesn't take much common sense to see that reforming welfare, as important as this is, will affect only about 2.5 percent of our federal spending, while reforming health care, whose rising costs have raised Medicare and Medicaid payments alone to more than 13 percent of our federal budget, is a far more serious problem that should be given priority.[20] Similarly, it requires little insight to see that a Congress willing to allocate billions of dollars for new prisons but only a fraction of that to create new jobs is trying to cure the symptoms of slow growth, not its causes. Those who propose raising our military spending, including a new Star Wars missile defense, ignore our underinvestment in day-care centers, libraries, early education, and R&D, all of which would help us grow, while rising military expenditures might provide employment in certain districts but will not strengthen our economy over time.

But our favorite fantasy is that if we reduce the size of government, prosperity will return, even though we no longer have a fertile frontier to exploit or a monopoly on the fast-growing mass-production and distribution industries that spearheaded growth. Free markets are efficient ways to distribute goods and services, but they won't re-create the huge advantages we have lost. Privatization of government services from sanitation to waste management is a productive reform that should continue, but for practical reasons, not ideological ones.

Our ideology of minimal government and self-reliance arose, as we have seen, from an economic environment that favored such beliefs. But to pay too much respect to the ideological slogans of our abundant past will only inhibit our search for answers today. The politicians' ongoing celebrations of frontier virtues in a time of restricted opportunity will only provoke an already angry nation. To extol family values when many American families cannot afford a decent life permits us to scold unwed mothers and errant fathers when we should be thinking of how to increase production and family incomes. When we self-righteously call for greater responsibility on the part of people who can't afford to pay for heat and light, we encourage ourselves to think that poor people themselves are the cause of our government deficits and stagnating wages. By cutting taxes despite high federal deficits, we implicitly blame big government, corrupt politicians, and fat-cat lobbyists for our plight. By raising military expenditures, we try to delude ourselves that our real enemy is external, when the enemy is increasingly ourselves as we continue to deny the causes of our recurring symptoms.

It was not such ideological reactions to our problems that restored our national confidence and prosperity time and again in our earlier history, but the dependable return of rapid growth in an economy propelled by its two great frontiers.

Even if we intelligently do everything we can to reverse our fortunes, the rate of productivity may grow only three or four tenths of a percent a year faster than it has since the early 1970s, significant over time but not enough to relieve the relentless pressure on our resources. Rather, our renewal will require that we now struggle continually to invest adequately in ourselves, and to sustain our optimism and political convictions without the abundant resources of our once-affluent society. This is the prospect that most Americans and their elected representatives won't face as they continue to look for an easy way out.

=

Because we are so disoriented by the long interruption in our material progress, we often ignore our genuine strengths. We are still the most productive and richest nation per capita in the world, with unmatched reserves of financial resources and productive capacity.[21] We remain leaders in dozens of key industries, from chemicals to electric turbines, personal computers and software, semiconductors and biotechnology. We are the best retailers and distributors in the world. We are an entrepreneurial people and a mobile one, a sprawling nation with plenty of room for new beginnings. Unlike the world's former economic leaders, such as Holland and England, we are still a gigantic marketplace where the world's best companies continue to build plants and distribution facilities. We are aging far less quickly than our advanced competitors, for whom the financial pressure of Social Security and

pension obligations will be even greater than ours. Our high
levels of immigration, if periodically overwhelming, are a
source of young, ambitious people, whose predecessors
throughout our history have been highly successful here, no
matter how they may have been insulted for genetic incapac-
ities by the "experts" of the day. We are still one of the best-
educated peoples in the world.

Yet we are unable to marshal these advantages. Even when
we achieve consensus, as in the case of rising health-care
costs, for example, we don't sustain our convictions long
enough to act firmly. Instead, such stubborn problems recede
from public discourse when we find we can't solve them, often
to be replaced by yet another set of concerns. By the fall of
1994 health care, once high on our list of problems, was dis-
placed, when we learned that there was no easy solution, by
fear of crime and the clamor to reform welfare, which may
also prove to be politically insoluble.[22] As noted, we treat our
symptoms and ignore their causes. In the meantime our frustration rises.

=

This has not always been the American way. Our ideology
was tempered by pragmatism throughout most of our
history. Though we distrusted government, most Americans
happily agreed to subsidize canals, roads, schools, and the
land-grant universities so important to our technological
leadership. We willingly paid for local government to establish law and order in the rough-and-tumble West, and to help

run our complex cities. For all our proud individualism, our private corporations led the world in investment, experimentation, and the willingness to take risks, not by stressing small entrepreneurial ventures, as valuable as they are, but by erecting giant bureaucratic enterprises. While we often spoke romantically about our self-reliance, we were usually willing to conform if it paid. Workers in America submitted more readily than those of other nations to the rigors of the assembly line for the sake of a good paycheck. In fact, as our nation got richer, fewer of us worked for ourselves. Only 12.5 percent of us are now self-employed, compared with 21.5 percent in 1910.[23] Our ideologies also exaggerate the strength of the nuclear family. Unlike those in Europe, American families dispersed quickly in search of economic opportunity.[24]

For our American ancestors, equality and democracy were not incontrovertible ideological principles learned from a textbook but new beliefs that helped organize a changing society. Because the old-line Federalists feared mob rule—which some members of Congress now virtually advocate by means of electronically interactive referenda—universal suffrage for white males had to be wrested from the ruling elite by the self-made men of the 1820s. Even Jefferson was concerned near his death that democracy might have gone too far.[25] A generation later the poet Walt Whitman wondered what it was that could hold our diverse and unstructured country together.[26] The answer of course was democracy, which fostered economic growth, and in turn deepened our loyalty to its principles by protecting our rights to our property and a free education, as well as to compete with others on an equal basis and to take entrepreneurial risk without fear of landing in a debtors' prison.

Slow economic growth has now weakened this pragmatic spirit. Our greatest vitality now resides largely at local and regional levels where private enterprise and government often work imaginatively together, where citizens are closer to their problems and can readily see the results of their reforms and of their taxes, and where ideology is less paralyzing than it is in Washington. But we cannot expect local government to protect our hard-won civil rights, take care of the poor, or maintain our national defense. Local governments cannot build national highways, oversee far-flung corporations, or even help coordinate an electronic superhighway. Solutions at local levels will play an important role in any renewal of America, but many of the problems that beset us are nation-wide in scope. To relinquish some of our most cherished rights to local authorities could be dangerous indeed.

=

Some believe that because we are still the richest people in the world we can cope with slow growth. But history turns less on absolute economic conditions than on expectations, self-esteem, and a people's sense of fairness. Our high standard of living as compared with those of our Old World ancestors will not cushion us forever against persistent disappointment. It is absurd, for example, to tell twenty-year-olds who doubt they will ever be able to buy a house like the one

they grew up in that they eat better than Louis XIV ever did![27]
Slow economic growth is especially dangerous because without a steep depression or spectacular unemployment rates it
conceals the accumulating damage. Nations decline whimper
by whimper.

Slow economic growth may increasingly set old pensioners against young workers, homeowners against renters, suburbs against cities, natives against immigrants, light-skinned
Americans against dark-skinned ones, debtors against credi-
tors, and those with power, by virtue of their own wealth or
their paid representation in Washington, against those who
have none. We have seen much of this already in the angry arguments over affirmative action, immigration, school curricula, capital punishment, the costs of welfare, Social Security,
protecting the environment, and the government's role in
health care. Once, equality meant that we could all get ahead.
For too many of us, equality now means having to give something up.

Yet, economically, we are, as we have seen, in the same situation as other advanced nations. We are all subject to the
same competitive pressures, including fragmenting markets
and falling returns on investment. Our main rival, however, is
not the rest of the world, it is the memory of our exceptional
past, when our economic advantages made us the most productive country in every major industry and our incomes
grew accordingly, and when the world came to our door to
borrow money. The trouble with trying to recapture our past
by conjuring up its ideological form again is that we falsify our

history for the sake of easy answers, all the while denying our present conditions. Until we acknowledge the fundamental change in our circumstances, see that our problems are not primarily moral and ideological, and reduce our fear of a world in which we can no longer count on constant rapid material gain, we cannot begin to seek workable solutions. We may ultimately abandon our most cherished political convictions, and this would be a disaster. Throughout our history we believed that we were a chosen people, a belief essentially sustained by our growing affluence. Now, we shall see who we are without it.

NOTES

CHAPTER 1. TWO DECADES OF SLOW GROWTH

1. Long-term growth data from Angus Maddison, *Dynamic Forces in Capitalist Development* (Oxford: Oxford University Press, 1991), p. 50. All modern growth data for the U.S. economy are derived from *The National Income and Product Accounts of the United States,* published by the Bureau of Economic Analysis (BEA) of the Department of Commerce. Real gross domestic product (GDP) is calculated in 1987 dollars. The growth rate from 1973 to 1993 is calculated from year-end 1973, which was an approximate peak in economic activity.

2. These estimates were based on a reduction in the rate of growth of an average 1 percent a year. Interest rates, labor participation rates, and the savings rate were held unchanged. Changes in wages, family incomes, corporate profits, and state and local tax revenues were assumed to fall proportionately. The calculations were made with the help of the econometric forecasting company Data Resources Inc. of Lexington, Mass.

3. Mortgage Bankers Association and Commerce Department estimates. See also *Pocket Chartroom,* Goldman Sachs & Co., November 1994.

4. Interview with author, May 1993 and March 1995.

5. *National Income and Product Accounts,* Bureau of Economic Analysis, Department of Commerce.

6. For the Federal Reserve's thinking, see "Why Policy Makers at the Fed Want Strong Economic Growth to Slow Down," *Wall Street Journal,* November 14, 1994.

7. Based on assumptions detailed in note 2. Calculations by Data Resources Inc.

8. BEA. Long-term GDP per capita from Maddison, op. cit., p. 49. The unusually sharp economic contractions before and after World War I kept average growth rates low over the years, but even so they rose above their current levels by the mid-1920s.

9. Maddison, op. cit., p. 50.

10. Ibid., p. 51. Paul A. David, "The Growth of Real Product Before 1840: New Evidence, Controlled Conjectures," *Journal of Economic History,* June 1967. David's long-term estimates of productivity are summarized in Moses Abramovitz, "The Search for the Sources of Growth: Areas of Ignorance, Old and New," *Journal of Economic History,* June 1993. See also John W. Kendrick, *Productivity Trends in the United States* (Princeton: National Bureau of Economic Research, 1961).

11. Modern productivity data from the Bureau of Labor Statistics (BLS) of the Labor Department. Historical comparison based on Paul David., op. cit., and in an interview with Mr. David, February 6, 1995.

12. Maddison, op. cit., p. 131.

13. For example, in 1979, 38 percent of high school graduates between twenty-five and thirty-four worked in manufacturing. By 1987 the proportion fell to 29 percent. Meanwhile those who worked in wholesale and retail jobs rose from 18 percent to 23 percent. Frank Levy and Richard J. Murnane, "U.S. Earnings Levels and Earnings Inequality: A Review of Recent Trends and Proposed Explanations," *Journal of Economic Literature,* September 1992. This is one of the best summaries of research on the decline of wages and the redistribution of income. On the issue of the shift from high-paying to low-paying jobs, see also Barry Bluestone and Bennett Harrison, *The Deindustrialization of America* (New York: Basic Books, 1982), and Lawrence F. Katz and Kevin M. Murphy, "Changes in Relative Wages, 1963–1987: Supply and Demand Factors," *Quarterly Journal of Economics,* February 1992.

14. All measures of compensation show either that average wages have fallen or that at best they are rising only slightly and at a rate far below their historical average. The most commonly cited measure of earnings is "Average Weekly Earnings," 1993 dollars, Current Employment Statistics, BLS. It includes the

earnings of about 80 percent of workers in America. Some analysts have criticized the usefulness of such wage data because they do not include the rise in pension and especially health insurance benefits. In fact, including these benefits makes little difference once they are properly discounted for inflation. Due to the rapid health cost inflation, health insurance benefits after inflation rose only marginally in the 1980s. Pension benefits on balance declined over these years.

The BLS computes an Employment Cost Index (ECI) going back to 1979 that includes wages and salaries for all workers, supervisory and nonsupervisory alike, plus benefits. Including benefits and the faster rising income of the 20 percent or so of workers who are supervisory or managerial does raise average compensation marginally over these years, but still at a rate of growth that is almost inconsequential compared with our historical record over virtually any other twenty-year period. Estimates of the compensation of the typical (median) worker, however, still show a decline in compensation even when including benefits. (I suspect health benefits are not properly discounted for inflation, which if done would reduce real compensation still more.) Estimates of the income of minority workers, young workers, and those with only a high school education show a sharp decline in mean and median compensation over these years (see Chapter 5).

Some analysts believe that, health insurance aside, inflation for other purchases has been overstated over these years. If so, real wages rose more quickly than the official data suggest, if again far below the historical rate. It should be remembered that one reason inflation may be lower is that consumers have defensively shifted their purchases of goods to cheaper items—everything from discounted clothing to generic products. They may also travel farther to shop or spend more time looking for bargains. To the extent that for a lower rate of inflation, it should not be construed as an improvement in the standard of living. The BEA has derived several adjusted measures of inflation, but even when a lower rate of inflation is used to discount wages, all measures of compensation growth essentially fell or grew only marginally over these years. Moreover, some economists contend that the composition of employment by industries has shifted in such a way as to make the methods for computing wages and salaries overstate their rise, and that government data require significant revisions (Lawrence Mishel and Jared Bernstein, *The State of Working America 1994–95* [Washington, D.C.: Economic Policy Institute, 1994], pp. 109–13).

After examining all the available measures of employee compensation, a 1994 Commerce and Labor commission succinctly concludes that all measures of income growth produce the same sorry results. Income has risen far more slowly than it once did. "They tell the same story," the researchers write. *Fact Finding Report,* Commission on the Future of Worker-Management Relations, Departments of Commerce and Labor, 1994, p. 19.

15. Mishel and Bernstein, op. cit., pp. 26, 138.

16. Robert A. Margo, *The Labor Force in the Nineteenth Century,* National Bureau of Economic Research, 1992. Also, Margo and Georgia C. Villaflor, "The Growth of Wages in Antebellum America: New Evidence," *Journal of Economic History,* December 1987. Margo and Villaflor found that wages fluctuated sharply, but that they rose inexorably over the century. The data for real wages for the twentieth century are more straightforward. See the *Historical Statistics of the United States,* Bureau of the Census. Also see Claudia Goldin, *Labor Markets in the Twentieth Century,* National Bureau of Economic Research, 1993.

17. These are based on the same assumptions as in note 2.

18. Paul Bairoch, "International Industrialization Levels from 1750 to 1980," *Journal of European Economic History,* Spring 1982, pp. 294–95.

19. In 1985 U.S. dollars. Maddison, op. cit., pp. 6–7.

20. Maddison, p. 99. Christina D. Romer has refined this analysis, but her estimates of long-term economic growth remain essentially the same as Maddison's. See "Remeasuring Business Cycles," working paper, University of California, Berkeley, January 1994. Also, Romer, "The Prewar Business Cycle Reconsidered: New Estimates of Gross National Product, 1869–1908," *Journal of Political Economy,* February 1989.

21. BEA data. Romer finds that pre–World War II recessions were somewhat less harsh than formerly believed; nevertheless, the average post–World War II recession was still more mild on average than prewar recessions, if less so. Romer, "Remeasuring Business Cycles."

22. Maddison, op. cit., pp. 49–51.

23. Frederick Jackson Turner, "The Significance of the Frontier in American History," a paper read at the American Historical Association, July 12, 1893, from *The Frontier in American History* (Tucson: University of Arizona Press, 1986), pp. 37–38.

24. Ibid., pp. 32, 37.

25. Gordon S. Wood, *The Radicalism of the American Revolution* (New York: Alfred A. Knopf, 1992), pp. 309, 311.

26. Richard Hofstadter, *The American Political Tradition* (New York: Vintage, 1989), p. 40.

27. Charles Sellers, *The Market Revolution, Jacksonian America, 1815–1846* (New York: Oxford University Press, 1991), p. 239.

28. Calhoun quoted by Turner, op. cit., p. 2, as well as Wood. On Americans in cities, Wood, op. cit., pp. 309–10.

29. Sellers, op. cit., p. 5.

30. Wood, op. cit., pp. 122–23. In Hanoverian England, for example, Wood writes that half the population was at one time or other dependent on "charity for subsistence."

31. Gary M. Walton and Roger LeRoy Miller, *Economic Issues in American History* (San Francisco: Canfield Press, 1978), p. 67.

32. Alice Hanson Jones concluded that real per capita income was higher in America in 1774 than in the leading economies of the time, England, Holland, and France. Jones, *Wealth of a Nation to Be* (New York: Columbia University Press, 1980), p. 303. "I conclude the level of living attained on the eve of the American Revolution by the typical free colonist, even the 'Poor' one, was substantial," p. 340.

33. Turner, "Contributions of the West to American Democracy," *Atlantic Monthly,* January 1903, from *The Frontier in American History,* p. 259.

34. Calvin Colton, *Junius Tracts, VII: Capital and Labor* (New York, 1844), p. 15, quoted by Sellers, op. cit., p. 238.

35. See, especially, Alexander Keyssar, *Out of Work: The First Century of Unemployment in Massachusetts* (Cambridge: Cambridge Univeristy Press, 1986). This book documents the American reluctance to concede that there were high numbers of unemployed through no fault of their own.

36. See in general John Mack Faragher, *Daniel Boone: The Life and Legend of an American Pioneer* (New York: Henry Holt & Co., 1992).

37. Wood., op. cit., p. 309.

38. Faragher, op. cit., especially pp. 246–49.

39. Ibid., pp. 294–300.

40. Contrary to previously held views, economic historians in the last generation have discovered that the American economy grew fairly rapidly in the first half of the nineteenth century. See, especially, David, op. cit., Margo, op. cit., and Hanson, op. cit. Thomas Weiss revised David's estimates, but his work also shows a rapid rise in the rate of growth in the first half of the nineteenth century. Weiss, "U.S. Labor Force Estimates and Economic Growth 1800–1860," in Robert Gallman and John Wallis, *American Economic Growth and the Standard of Living Before the Civil War* (Chicago: University of Chicago Press, 1994). For a

good general summary of the research on economic growth, see Susan P. Lee and Peter Passell, *A New Economic View of American History* (New York: W. W. Norton & Co., 1979).

41. Colonialist Charles Carrol, quoted by Wood, op. cit., p. 134.

42. Robert D. Mitchell, *Commercialism and Frontier: Perspectives on the Early Shenandoah Valley* (Charlottesville: University Press of Virginia, 1977). Quoted by Sellers, op. cit., p. 15.

43. See Sellers in general, op. cit., pp. 14–19.

44. Wood, op. cit., p. 314. Sellers, op. cit., pp. 22, 25. Hofstadter, op. cit., p. 52.

45. Sellers, op. cit., p. 391. George Rogers Taylor, *The Transportation Revolution* (Armonk, N.Y.: M. E. Sharpe, 1951).

46. David, op. cit. See Weiss, op. cit., for a summary of his and David's estimates, p. 27.

47. George Rogers Taylor and Irene D. Neu, *The American Railroad Network* (Cambridge: Harvard University Press, 1956), especially p. 49.

48. Margo, *Labor Force*, p. 8; *Historical Statistics of the United States*, Bureau of the Census, Washington, D.C.

49. Richard R. Nelson and Gavin Wright, "The Rise and Fall of American Technological Leadership: The Postwar Era in Historical Perspective," *Journal of Economic Literature*, December 1992, especially p. 1931.

50. Margo, *Labor Force*, pp. 30–37. For the struggle of workers earlier in the nineteenth century, see Sellers, op. cit., pp. 332–63. On the rising inequality of income in the nineteenth century, see Jeffrey G. Williamson and Peter H. Lindert, *American Inequality: A Macroeconomic History* (New York: Academic Press, 1980). Also, Margo's revisions and critique, "Historical Trends in the Distribution of Wages: The American Case," a speech given at the University of Pennsylvania, 1993. Margo finds that inequality did not grow as severely as Williamson and Lindert maintain.

A great deal of scholarship has been devoted to explain why the labor union movement was weaker in America than in Europe. Many Americans, especially immigrants, suffered in these years. Women and child labor and politically weak immigrant groups were abused. The courts and the strong arm of the law often took sides against organized labor. Yet there was no social democratic political party allied with labor in America as there is throughout Europe. Werner Sombart, a German economist, asked in a famous essay written in 1906, "Why Is There No Socialism in the United States?" Some modern historians have demonstrated that there was at least some degree of class consciousness in these years. For example, see Sean Wilentz, *Chants Democratic: New York City and the Rise of the American Working Class* (New York: Oxford University Press, 1984). Labor unions and reform movements clearly made important contributions not only in raising workers' incomes but also in pressing for public education and in other matters. But, overall, it was rapid economic growth that assuaged America's young, struggling population. Spreading economic opportunity provided a sufficient safety valve to vent discontent and offset the level of abuse, a safety valve that was less available or reliable in Europe. See earlier scholars such as John Commons, et al., *History of Labour in the United States* (Macmillan, 1936), and, in particular, Selig Perlman and Philip Taft, *History of Labor in the United States, 1896 to 1932.* Sombart comes to a similar conclusion. See also Hofstadter, op. cit., p. 113, who uses Turner's phrase, "safety valve," to describe how a strong economy influenced nineteenth-century Americans. As he writes, "it was far easier to reconcile the Northern masses to the profit system than [John] Calhoun would ever admit."

51. Charles A. Beard and Mary R. Beard, *The American Spirit* (New York: Macmillan, 1942), pp. 332, 383.

52. Margo, op. cit., p. 15.

53. Timothy J. Hatton and Jeffrey G. Williamson, "International Migration and World Development: A Historical Perspective," Discussion Paper 1606, Harvard University, 1992, p. 53.

54. On the Depression's pessimists, most notably the future Keynesian Alvin Hansen, see Alan Brinkley, *The End of Reform* (New York: Alfred A. Knopf, 1995), p. 131–35. For growth data, National Income and Product Accounts, BEA. Productivity data, BLS.

55. Herman Kahn, William Pfaf, and Anthony J. Wiener, eds., *American Academy of Arts and Sciences Commission on the Year 2000.* New York, Hudson Institute, 1967. Cited by Paul Krugman, *The Age of Diminished Expectations* (Cambridge: MIT Press, 1992), p. 195. As Krugman points out, the worst case that Kahn anticipated was that productivity would grow at 2.5 percent a year.

56. Samuel Bowles, David M. Gordon, and Thomas E. Weisskopf, *Beyond the Waste Land* (New York: Doubleday, 1983), pp. 75–97.

CHAPTER 2. WHAT WE HAD

1. Jones, op. cit., p. 303. Gary M. Walton and Hugh Rockoff summarize the research: "By most any standard of comparison, the quality of life and standards of material well-being were extraordinarily high for free Americans by the end

of the Colonial period" (*The History of the American Economy* [New York: Harcourt, Brace & World, 1964]), p. 99.

2. Kenneth L. Sokoloff and Georgia C. Villaflor, "The Early Achievement of Modern Stature in America," *Social Science History,* Fall 1982. Robert William Fogel, "Nutrition and the Decline of Mortality Since 1700: Some Preliminary Findings," from Stanley L. Engerman and Robert E. Gallman, *Long-term Factors in American Economic Growth* (Chicago: University of Chicago Press, 1986). For a summary of the literature on health and economic conditions, see Richard H. Steckel, "Stature and the Standard of Living," Ohio State University, January 1995.

3. The profitability of slave labor demonstrates how valuable it was for our exports. See R. Evans, Jr., on the profitability of slavery, "The Economics of American Negro Slavery," in *Aspects of Labor Economics* (Princeton University Press, 1962). See Yasukichi Yasuba for a novel, sophisticated analysis of the value of slavery, "The Profitability and Viability of Plantation Slavery in the United States," cited by Lee and Passell, op. cit., p. 169.

The most likely case, I think, is that abusively cheap slave labor helped early growth in America enormously by making it possible to produce inexpensive tobacco and then cotton exports. Eventually, slavery was self-defeating, however, because by not building a solid working middle class, the South restricted its ability to develop a strong market for goods. Such a working class would have been able to support the sort of manufacturing economy that the South is only recently beginning to develop. As some economists have also pointed out, the high if temporary investment in slavery blocked the development of new manufacturing industries. Developing countries today that depend on very cheap labor may someday find themselves in the same situation if they don't raise wages adequately in order to create a strong domestic market of their own, a transformation that probably would require democratizing their governments in ways some of them will continue to resist.

4. Richard R. Nelson and Gavin Wright, "The Rise and Fall of American Technological Leadership: The Postwar Era in Historical Perspective," *Journal of Economic Literature,* December 1992, p. 1935.

5. These conclusions derive from many sources. But nowhere is the argument better summarized than in Nelson and Wright, op. cit. See, especially, p. 1935.

6. On European mass production, Nelson and Wright, op. cit., p. 1937, write that "by the end of the nineteenth century, American industry assumed a qualitatively different place in the world."

7. Maddison, op. cit., pp. 49–51.

8. Ibid.

9. In general, see Moses Abramovitz, "Catching Up, Forging Ahead, and Falling Behind," *Journal of Economic History,* June 1986.

10. Though the arguments in this book depart from those made by Nelson and Wright, the authors put the question this way: "How can policies respond appropriately to 'what we have lost' without a clear knowledge of what it was that we had and how we got it?" Op. cit., p. 1932.

11. Alfred D. Chandler, Jr., *Scale and Scope: The Dynamics of Industrial Capitalism* (Cambridge: Belknap Press, 1990), p. 251, also pp. 235–97 in general.

12. Taylor, op. cit., p. 32.

13. Alfred D. Chandler, *The Visible Hand: The Managerial Revolution in American Business* (Cambridge: Belknap Press, 1977), pp. 82–86.

14. Taylor and Neu, op. cit., p. 3.

15. Ibid., p. 49.

16. Chandler, *Visible Hand,* pp. 88–89.

17. Ibid., p. 171. On the development of the great railroad systems, which were typically built in the 1870s and in the 1880s through acquisitions, see Chandler in general, pp. 148–71.

18. Taylor and Neu, op. cit., p. 2.

19. On nineteenth-century future shock, consider what Henry Adams wrote: "The nineteenth century moved fast and furious, so that one who moved in it felt sometimes giddy, watching it spin. . . ." (*Mont-Saint-Michel and Chartres* [New York: Penguin Classics, 1986], p. 35).

20. Chandler, *Scale and Scope,* pp. 52, 53. Maddison, op. cit., pp. 198–99.

21. Chandler, *Visible Hand,* pp. 249–50. See in general Richard B. Tennant, *The American Cigarette Industry* (New Haven: Yale University Press, 1950).

22. Chandler, *Visible Hand,* pp. 250–53. On the "disassembly" line, see David A. Hounshell, *From the American System to Mass Production 1800–1932* (Baltimore: Johns Hopkins University Press, 1984), p. 10.

23. Harold F. Williamson and Arnold R. Daum, *The American Petroleum Industry: The Age of Illumination, 1859–1899* (Evanston: Northwestern University Press, 1959), p. 282. Quoted by Chandler, op. cit., p. 256.

24. Peter Temin, *Iron and Steel in Nineteenth-Century America: An Economic Inquiry* (Cambridge: MIT Press), p. 165.

25. Chandler, *Scale and Scope,* p. 129.

26. See in general Albert Fishlow, "Productivity and Technological Change in the Railroad Sector," in *Output, Employment and Productivity in the United States After 1800* (New York: National Bureau of Economic Research, 1966).

27. Chandler, *Visible Hand*, p. 236. Harold Barger, *Distribution's Place in the American Economy Since 1869* (Princeton: Princeton University Press, 1955).

28. See in particular Chandler, *Visible Hand*, pp. 244–48. See in general John William Ferry, *A History of the Department Store* (New York: Macmillan, 1960).

29. Chandler, *Visible Hand*, pp. 287–314.

30. Nelson and Wright, op. cit., pp. 1940–41. Chandler, *Visible Hand*, pp. 272–81. Michael Best, *The New Competition, Institutions of Industrial Restructuring* (Cambridge: Harvard University Press, 1990), pp. 55–58. On the distinction of American management compared with that of other countries, see Bruce Kogut, "National Organizing Principles of Work and the Erstwhile Dominance of the American Multinational Corporation," in *Industrial and Corporate Change*, 1992.

31. On the difficulty Ford had in retaining workers despite high wages, see Daniel M. G. Raff, "Wage Determination Theory and the Five-Dollar Day at Ford," *Journal of Economic History*, June 1988. Also, Hounshell, op. cit., pp. 11, 257.

32. See especially Nathan Rosenberg, *Inside the Black Box: Technology and Economics* (Cambridge: Cambridge University Press, 1982). Also, a classic study on the subject, Kenneth Arrow, "The Economic Implications of Learning by Doing," *Economic Studies*, June 1962. Also, Nelson and Wright, op. cit., p. 1935.

33. Nelson and Wright, op. cit., p. 1937. For an important paper on the theoretical underpinnings, see Paul R. Romer, "Increasing Returns and Long Run Growth," *Journal of Political Economy*, October 1986.

34. The British had trouble adopting the so-called American factory system, already well developed by mid-century in the firearms industry. This was not mass production as we now know it but a sort of first stage in which the interchangeability of parts made production faster and routine. British consumers did not want firearms that were exactly the same, however. They were accustomed to custom-made, distinctive products. This unwillingness to buy similar products over the years probably significantly retarded the development of mass production overseas in general. See Lee and Passell, op cit., p. 99.

35. Margo, *Labor Force*, Table 3.

36. Margo, "The Incidence and Duration of Unemployment: Some Long-term Comparisons," *Economics Letters*, March 1990. Stanley Engerman and Claudia

Goldin, "Seasonality in Nineteenth-Century Labor Markets," working paper (Cambridge: National Bureau of Economic Research, December 1991). Also see Goldin in general, *Labor Market in Twentieth Century.*

37. Best, op. cit., pp. 50–51.

38. Examination of letters and local newspaper articles in Europe shows that even the relatively poor were well informed about real economic conditions in America. During recessions, for example, the flow of immigration abated. See J. D. Gould, "European Inter-Continental Emigration 1815–1914, Patterns and Causes," *Journal of European Economic History,* Winter 1979.

39. Hounshell, op. cit., p. 224. Chandler, *Visible Hand,* p. 280.

40. See Raff, op. cit., on Ford's $5-a-day wage.

41. The proportion of factories using electricity rose from 25 percent in 1910 to 75 percent in 1930 (Warren D. Devine, Jr., "From Shafts to Wires: Historical Perspectives on Electrification," *Journal of Economic History,* June 1983). The proportion of urban families with electricity rose from 33 percent in 1909 to 96 percent in 1939 (Stanley Lebergott, *The American Economy: Income, Wealth and Want* [Princeton: Princeton University Press, 1976]). Both quoted by Nelson and Wright, op. cit., p. 1945. For car and washing-machine ownership, see Stanley Lebergott, *Pursuing Happiness: American Consumers in the Twentieth Century* (Princeton: Princeton University Press, 1993), pp. 131, 113.

42. See in general Gavin Wright, "The Origins of American Industrial Success, 1879–1940," *American Economic Review,* September 1990.

43. Ibid., p. 661.

44. Chandler, *Visible Hand,* pp. 348, 482–83. Chandler carefully shows how almost all of these companies were capital-intensive and dependent on large markets and economies of scale.

45. Between 1950 and 1970, for example, the chemical industry grew about two and a half times faster than did the GNP. Alfred Chandler, a working paper, "Global Enterprises—Big Business and the Wealth of Nations, The United States, 1880s–1980s," November 1993, p. 36.

46. The productivity of the railroads, and the new wholesalers, department stores, and retail chains, among others, all benefited greatly from new technologies and the growing economies of scale, as we have seen. In the immediate postwar years, everything from the jet to fast-food chains and TV marketing raised the productivity of services. It can be determined that services productivity in general rose fairly rapidly over these years by comparing historical

growth rates of manufacturing productivity with productivity for the overall economy. The remainder, roughly speaking, is the growth in services productivity. From the data compiled by Paul David in the nineteenth century and by the Commerce Department in the twentieth century, it is clear that services productivity rose rapidly in the nineteenth century and most of the twentieth century. In the past two decades, however, its growth slowed dramatically. For the post–World War II period, see William J. Baumol, Sue Anne Batey Blackman, and Edward N. Wolff, *Productivity and American Leadership* (Cambridge: MIT Press, 1991), pp. 72–82. What complicates matters is that as products become more complex, manufacturing utilizes many more services in production, which means that we may overestimate productivity in manufacturing. But even taking this into account, the reduction in services productivity growth is substantial compared with pre-1973 rates of growth. See also Frank Levy, *Dollars and Dreams: The Changing American Income Distribution* (New York: W. W. Norton & Co., 1988), pp. 82–84, on why the shift to services does not matter as much as is widely believed.

47. Even if manufacturing productivity grows as much as 2 percent to 3 percent a year faster than services productivity, a far wider margin than has been historically true, a shift of 10 percent to 12 percent of our sales from manufacturing to services would reduce productivity growth by a range of only .2 percent to a maximum of .36 percent a year.

48. Best, op. cit., p. 63.

49. Chandler, *Visible Hand,* pp. 374–75.

50. For the definitive work on how workers fare in large corporations compared with those in small companies, see Charles Brown, James Hamilton, and James Medoff, *Employers Large and Small* (Cambridge: Harvard University Press, 1990). For a debunking of the idea that small corporations create most of our jobs, see Bennett Harrison, *Lean and Mean: The Changing Landscape of Corporate Power in the Age of Flexibility* (New York: Basic Books, 1994), pp. 37–52. On innovation in large and small firms, also see Harrison, pp. 53, 74. The capital intensity of mass-production giants has been discussed and is well documented in Chandler, *Visible Hand* and the working paper "Global Enterprises."

51. Peter Drucker, the management writer, called mass production "an economic doctrine as well as an approach to manufacture." Quoted by Hounshell, op. cit., p. 10.

52. Walter Kiechell III, "The Decline of the Experience Curve," *Fortune,* October 5, 1981. Quoted by William J. Abernathy, Kim B. Clark, and Alan M. Kantrow, *Industrial Renaissance, Producing a Competitive Future for America* (New York: Basic Books, 1983), p. 19.

53. James P. Womack, Daniel T. Jones, and Daniel Roos, *The Machine That Changed the World: The Story of Lean Production* (New York: Rawson, 1990), p. 43.

54. Chandler, *Visible Hand,* pp. 371, 483.

CHAPTER 3. WHAT WE LOST

1. See Chapter 1, p. 34.

2. The classic book on the economic aftermath of the Treaty of Versailles is John Maynard Keynes, *The Economic Consequences of the Peace* (New York: Harcourt, Brace & Young, 1920). On tariffs and trade restriction during the Depression, see Charles P. Kindleberger, *The World in Depression 1929–1939* (Berkeley: University of California Press, 1973). Also, John A. Garraty, *The Great Depression* (New York: Doubleday, 1987). On the reaction at Bretton Woods to former unstable exchange rates, see Kindleberger, pp. 293–94.

3. *Encyclopaedia Britannica,* "International Trade," 1973, p. 140.

4. Wright, op. cit., pp. 663–64.

5. Richard Auty, "Materials Intensity of GDP," *Resources Policy,* December 1995. V. E. Spencer, *Raw Materials in the United States Economy, 1900–77.* Bureau of Census Technical Paper No. 47, Washington, D.C., 1980. Minerals alone accounted for 7 percent of GDP in 1900 and only 1.7 percent in 1977.

6. As Nelson and Wright write, "American manufacturing firms and their technologies not only were resources and capital intensive, but operated at much greater scale than did their counterparts in the United Kingdom and on the Continent." Nelson and Wright, op. cit., p. 1939. For a general discussion of mass production in the key European countries, see Michael J. Piore and Charles F. Sabel, *The Second Industrial Divide* (New York: Basic Books, 1984). On the specific inhibitions for British and German manufacturers, see in general Chandler, *Scale and Scope.*

7. Jeffrey D. Sachs and Howard J. Shatz, "Trade and Jobs in U.S. Manufacturing," working paper presented to Brookings Institution panel, April 1994, p. 12.

8. Samuel Bowles, David M. Gordon, and Thomas E. Weisskopf, *Beyond the Waste Land* (New York: Anchor Press, 1983), pp. 80–81.

9. Maddison, op. cit., pp. 50–53.

10. Ibid., p. 51.

11. U.S. Bureau of the Census, Foreign Trade Division, U.S. Merchandise Trade Report.

12. Maddison, op. cit., p. 53. To remain consistent, I have used the Maddison data, which ends in 1987. There has been no significant catch-up in productivity levels since then, except for Japan, which has probably closed the gap by a few additional percentage points.

13. A study by Morgan Guaranty Trust Co. finds that imports from Asia and Latin America accounted for 22 percent of all imports during the first three years of the 1980s recovery and expansion and 45 percent during the first three years of the 1990s recovery and expansion. A growing proportion of our capital-goods imports are coming from developing rather than developed nations as well. David Wessel, "U.S. Growth Benefits a New Set of Nations," *Wall Street Journal,* May 2, 1994. Also, John Markoff, "Where the Chips May Fall Next," *New York Times,* April 17, 1995.

14. Sachs and Shatz, op. cit., p. 13.

15. A widely read paper by Paul Krugman and Robert Lawrence helped correct the overriding impression that direct competition with low-wage producers accounted for most of our lost jobs and reduced wages. Essentially, they showed that at least in terms of direct effects, trade with such producers was simply too small to account for the damage done. "Trade, Jobs, and Wages," *Scientific American,* April 1994.

But many critics have found that Krugman and Lawrence have gone too far. In particular, see Sachs and Shatz, op. cit. Also see two prior papers, Lawrence Katz and Kevin Murphy, "Changes in Relative Wages, 1963–87: Supply and Demand Factors," in *Differences and Changes in Wage Structures* (Chicago: University of Chicago Press, 1994), and Richard Freeman, "Is Globalisation Impoverishing Low-Skill American Workers," Urban Institute, November 1993. Also, Edward E. Leamer, "Wage Effects of U.S.-Mexican Free Trade Agreement," from P. Garber, ed., *The Mexico-U.S. Free Trade Agreement* (Cambridge: MIT Press, 1993).

In my view, the central question is whether you can get any outcome other than what Lawrence and Krugman found if you only measure the direct effects of import competition, since our imports from low-wage nations, while rising rapidly, are small as a proportion of the total economy. The indirect effects of foreign competition are much harder if not impossible to measure statistically, yet they may be more potent than the direct effects. Once you assume that direct effects of imports are all that matters, I think it is virtually certain that you will come up with the conclusion that Lawrence and Krugman did. A creative attempt to measure the more important indirect effects of trade can be found in James K. Galbraith and Paulo Du Pin Calmon, "Industries, Trade and Wages," from Michael A. Bernstein and David Adler, eds., *Understanding American Economic Decline* (Cambridge: Cambridge University Press, 1994), pp. 161–98. My book argues that internationalization created a number of such indirect effects, including rising levels of uncertainty, greater instability, and business strategies to defend against foreign encroachment, which, in turn, led to reduced capital investment, reinforcing the declining trend in productivity and wage growth.

A second major factor, as we see in the rest of this chapter, is the relentless retreat throughout the world from traditional mass production to something more competitive and uncertain: flexible production and fragmenting markets.

In sum, I argue not that America slowed down simply because the rest of the advanced world speeded up, but that internationalization and fragmentation produced a network of consequences for American industries that went well beyond the direct effects of market share losses due to imports.

16. Though this book departs from many of its central conclusions, the classic work on this transformation is Piore and Sabel, op. cit. For a useful overview, see Zoltan J. Acs and David Audretsch, "The Restructuring of U.S. Markets," working draft, January 1986. A forerunner, though not a precise one, of the Piore and Sabel argument was made by Abernathy et al., *Industrial Renaissance*. The authors called the changes in manufacturing "de-maturity."

17. The average company employed 1,100 workers in 1967 and only 665 in 1985 (Harrison, op. cit., p. 37). Average GNP per firm also declined in the 1980s. Zoltan J. Acs and David S. Evans, "Entrepreneurship and Small Business Growth: A Case Study," from *Advances in the Study of Entrepreneurship, Innovation, and Economic Growth* (JAI Press, 1993). A statistical assessment of the rising level of competition since the early postwar period can be found in William G. Shepherd, "Causes of Increased Competition in the U.S. Economy, 1939–1980," *Review of Economics and Statistics,* April 1982.

18. According to IBM's "chief business strategist." Quoted in *The Economist,* "The Computer Industry Survey," February 27, 1993, p. 7.

19. On the flexible strategies of big business, see especially Harrison, op. cit., pp. 125–49.

20. *Ford Motor Co. State of the U.S. Automobile Industry* (Dearborn, Ford Motor, 1978). Cited by Abernathy et al., op. cit., p. 60.

21. The nation itself was slow to recognize the growing threat of overseas firms. Not until 1978 did America's balance of payments appear on a list of national goals. In that year, "an improved trade balance" was at last included in the Humphrey-Hawkins legislation as an explicit objective of American policy. Penelope Hartland-Thunberg, "The Political and Strategic Importance of Exports," U.S. Export Competitiveness Project, Washington, D.C., 1980, p. 32.

22. Womack et al., *The Machine That Changed the World,* op. cit., pp. 117–24.

23. On the electronic innovations for making production more flexible, especially the transfer machines of the 1920s and the evolution of numerically controlled machines in the 1970s, see Zoltan J. Acs, David B. Audretsch, and Bo Carlsson, "Flexible Technology and Firm Size," in *Small Business Economics,* Vol. 3, 1991, pp. 308–9. On the use of just-in-time inventorying and other managerial innovations in Japan, including utilizing workers, see Abernathy et al., op. cit., pp. 73–94. Also, Womack et al., op. cit., pp. 98–103 and pp. 142–53.

24. Womack, op. cit., p. 125.

25. Piore and Sabel, op. cit., pp. 133–64. Michael Storper, "Regional Worlds of Production: Learning and Innovation in the Technology Districts of France, Italy and the USA," *Regional Studies,* Vol. 27, May 1992. Also, Best, op. cit., pp. 201–26. On the efficiency of small firms, see Sang V. Nguyen and Arnold P. Reznek, "Returns to Scale in Small and Large U.S. Manufacturing Establishments," *Small Business Economics,* Vol. 3, 1991.

26. *New Product News,* Chicago, compilation done for the author, February 1994.

27. On steel, see Zoltan J. Acs, *The Changing Structure of the U.S. Economy* (New York: Praeger, 1984), pp. 210–12. On the chemical industry, see Chandler, "Global Enterprises," pp. 33–38.

28. See, for example, Jim Bessen, "Riding the Marketing Information Wave," *Harvard Business Review,* September–October 1993.

29. Piore and Sabel argue that the American consumer was satiated with mass-production goods by the 1970s. Op. cit., pp. 184–85. The economist Tibor Scitovsky wrote a book on the monotony of mass-production goods: *The Joyless Economy: The Psychology of Human Satisfaction* (Oxford: Oxford University Press), 1976. In my view, flexible production would have caught on eventually in America even without international competition as a response to the increasingly dissatisfied, bored consumer.

30. The best work I have seen on this is Daniel Luria, "A High Road Policy for U.S. Manufacturing," from C. Howes and A. Singh, *U.S. Industry, International Competitiveness, and Industrial Policy* (Ann Arbor: University of Michigan Press, 1994). Luria shows that the value added of small manufacturing firms is still lower than it is for large firms, as is productivity in general. This also helps explain why, as Medoff et al. have shown, small firms typically pay lower wages than do large firms. See also Luria, "Automation, markets and scale: Can flexible niching modernize US manufacturing?" *International Review of Applied Economics,* Vol. 4, 1990. Also, see in general Harrison, op. cit.

31. McKinsey Global Institute, "Productivity in the Processed Food Industry," *Manufacturing Productivity* (Washington, D.C.: McKinsey & Co., 1993), p. 4.

32. OECD national accounts. Robert Z. Lawrence found that in America the average rate of return was 18.73 percent between 1965 and 1969, 16.78 percent between 1970 and 1979, and 16.90 percent between 1980 and 1988 ("Time Horizons of American Management: The Role of Macroeconomic Factors," Council on Competitiveness, 1991, Table 8). But the rate of return in the United States remained higher than it was in most other advanced nations, suggesting that American companies are more reluctant to invest when returns go down. On the other hand, as a result, total profits in America grew more slowly.

33. Andrew Pollack, "A Back-to-Basics U-Turn in Japan," *New York Times*, August 26, 1994. George Stalk, Jr., and Alan M. Webber, "Japan's Dark Side of Time," *Harvard Business Review*, July–August 1993. Stalk and Webber point out that Toyota reduced its varieties of the Corolla from eleven to six, and Mazda cut 76 varieties from its 929 model.

34. Harrison, op. cit., "The Negative Competitive Consequences of Excessive Fragmentation: The Case of Prato," pp. 95–102.

35. As Dan Luria writes, "The loss of predictable demand and the advent of technologies that do not require large-scale operations have affected all market economies. Only in the U.S., however, are the results so stark and perverse." Luria, "High Road," p. 4. Luria is referring mostly to disparities in wages, but the observations apply to low levels of capital investment and hiring policies as well.

36. Ramchandran Jaikumar, "Postindustrial Manufacturing," *Harvard Business Review*, 1986, quoted by Best, op. cit., pp. 156–58. Best is also a consultant to business and has observed similar misuses of flexible technology among his clients. Interview with author, December 1, 1993.

37. Real interest rates—nominal rates less inflation—were generally higher in the 1980s in the United States (Lawrence, "Time Horizons," pp. 34–35). But real interest rates were lower in the 1970s in the United States compared with what they were overseas, and capital investment generally grew more rapidly in Europe and Japan. In fact, our capital-to-labor ratio has been falling fairly consistently since the 1950s no matter what the level of real rates. High real interest rates no doubt inhibited American capital investment in the 1980s. See Margaret M. Blair, "A Surprising Culprit Behind the Rush to Leverage," *The Brookings Review*, Winter 1989–90, pp. 19–26. But I would assign it less weight than others do for the reasons cited above.

38. Net nonresidential fixed investment (after depreciation) as a proportion of GDP (Data Resources Inc.).

39. The growth of gross nonresidential capital stock per worker. Maddison, op. cit., p. 142.

40. Nelson and Wright, op. cit., pp. 1952–53. National Science Foundation, *Science and Engineering Indicators* (Washington, D.C.: National Science Board, 1993), p. 100.

41. Commission on the Future of Worker-Management Relations, *Fact Finding Report* (Washington, D.C.: Departments of Labor and Commerce, 1994), p. 24.

42. Virginia L. du Rivage, ed., *New Policies for the Part-time and Contingent Workforce* (Armonk, N.Y.: M. E. Sharpe, 1992), pp. 17–22. Part-time workers earn on average about 60 percent of what full-time workers earn.

43. Report of the Commission on the Future of Worker-Management Relations, p. 17. This computation is based on the purchasing power parity indexes of the OECD.

44. On the "high-road" strategy of capital investment versus the "low-road" strategy of cutting wages, see Daniel Luria, "Where Good Jobs Come From: A Friendly Critique of Clintonomics," *American Prospect*, Fall 1994. Also, Luria, "High Road."

45. Jeffrey Williamson, "The Evolution of Global Labor Markets in the First and Second World Since 1830: Background Evidence and Hypotheses," Discussion Paper No. 1571, Harvard Institute of Economic Research, October 1991, p. 29. Williamson finds that, for example, in 1856 real wages in the United States were 94 percent higher than in Britain. In 1913 they were still 54 percent higher, despite the wave of immigration into America.

46. The insufficiency of aggregate demand gets almost no attention in the United States, partly because we are still living in a world that fears that too much demand will reignite inflation. See a European economist on the subject, Alain Liepitz, "New Tendencies in the International Division of Labor Regimes of Accumulation and Modes of Regulation," from Allen Scott and Michael Storper, *Production, Work, Territory* (London: Allen & Unwin, 1986), cited by Harrison, op. cit., p. 211.

47. The classic work on high wages as an incentive to invest is H. J. Habakkuk, *American and British Technology in the Nineteenth Century* (Cambridge: Cambridge University Press, 1962). For a summary of more current thinking on the subject, see Rosenberg, *Inside the Black Box,* pp. 15–21.

48. For a general discussion of this unresolved issue, see Harrison, op. cit., especially pp. 128–33. By contracting work out and forming networks with other companies, big firms may be able to become more flexible and retain the advantages of manufacturing, marketing, and distribution scales. But this will probably come at a cost.

49. Rates of return have generally risen slightly in recent years in advanced na-

tions, suggesting a retreat from the intensity of competition brought on by the worldwide recession and the willingness of labor to accept reductions in wages or modest increases. As economies expand cyclically, this will again probably reverse.

50. Sachs and Shatz, op. cit., p. 5.

51. Ibid., p. 6. The replacement of low-skilled workers with high-skilled workers has proceeded at a fairly steady rate since World War II. On whether or not there has been a "technology shock" in the 1980s and 1990s, also see Lawrence Mishel and Jared Bernstein, *Is the Technology Black Box Empty? An Empirical Examination of the Impact of Technology on Wage Inequality and the Employment Structure* (Washington, D.C., Economic Policy Institute, April 1994).

52. On whether lower wages in manufacturing influence wages in related services, see especially Galbraith and Calmon, op. cit., pp. 185–90. On switching to service jobs, see Jeff Groger and Eric Eide, "Changes in College Skills and the Rise in the College Wage Premium," working paper, University of California, San Francisco, 1992, cited by Frank Levy et al., "Education and Skills for the U.S. Work Force," *Aspen Institute Quarterly*, Winter 1994. Much of this hiring has been reversed since the late 1980s and over the course of the white-collar recession and its aftermath.

53. On the white-collar recession, Levy et al., op. cit., pp. 49–52. Mishel and Bernstein, *State of Working America*, p. 138. The authors found that salaries for college graduates began falling in 1987.

54. Commission on Worker-Management Relations, op. cit., p. 15.

55. Economic Report of the President, 1994, p. 117. Mishel and Bernstein, op. cit., p. 26. Some analysts argue that because the size of the average family is now smaller, these families are better off even though incomes have not risen on average. Family-income growth is mostly affected in the 1970s for adjustments in family size. In the 1980s, family income grew only .6 percent a year rather than .4 percent a year when adjusted for family size. However, families have reduced the number of children they have partly, if not largely, because they make less money. It is certainly odd to claim their standard of living has risen because they were not able to afford more children.

56. Bureau of the Census, Income, Poverty, and Health Insurance: 1993 (Washington, D.C.: Department of Commerce, 1994).

57. Joint Center for Housing Studies of Harvard University, *The State of the Nation's Housing*, Cambridge, 1994, p. 10.

58. Although we face the same competitive circumstances, for example, the distribution of income has remained significantly more equal in Europe than in

the United States. Another example of our differences is that governments in Europe sponsor much more nondefense R&D than the federal government in America does. In the United States, government R&D has been substantial but mostly for defense purposes. This is not necessarily to say that European solutions are always superior. Their unemployment rate is generally much higher than is America's, although their governmental support of the unemployed and their social net in general are more generous as well. Some of these issues will be addressed further in coming chapters.

CHAPTER 4. MISPLACED OPTIMISM

1. Henry Steele Commager, *The American Mind* (New Haven: Yale University Press, 1950), p. 5.

2. Thomas L. Friedman, "An American's Respite from Disillusionment," *New York Times,* September 19, 1993.

3. A Times Mirror Center Survey, reported in John H. Fund, "The Revolution of 1994," *Wall Street Journal,* October 19, 1994.

4. For example, see Alfred Kleinknecht, *Innovation Patterns in Crisis and Prosperity: Schumpeter's Long Cycle Reconsidered* (London: Macmillan, 1987). The author tallies what he considers dramatically important innovations as a way to explain changes in growth rates.

5. George Bancroft, *History of the Formation of the Constitution of the United States* (New York: D. Appleton & Co., 1882), p. 5.

6. Vannevar Bush, *Science, the Endless Frontier* (Washington, D.C.: Government Printing Office, 1945).

7. Robert W. Fogel, *Railroads and American Economic Growth: Essays in Econometric History* (Baltimore: Johns Hopkins University Press, 1970). See especially the summary, pp. 208–49. "The most important implication of this study," concludes Fogel, "is that no single innovation was vital for economic growth during the nineteenth century" (p. 234). He goes on: "The theory of overwhelming, singular innovations has probably been fostered by the modus operandi of competitive economies. Under competition firms tend to choose the most efficient of the available methods of production. Alternatives that could perform the same functions at somewhat greater cost are discarded and escape public attention. The absence from view of slightly less efficient processes creates the illusion that no alternatives exist. The illusion is heightened by the fact that the chosen process has an optimal set of institutional arrangements, appurtenances, and personnel."

8. For the history, see David, "Computer and Dynamo." But I think David's

general conclusion that the great productivity gains from computers are still to come suffers from the same overemphasis on a single technological break-through that Fogel so persuasively criticizes. Broader factors of competitiveness overwhelm any single technological innovation, no matter how grand.

9. Nelson and Wright, op. cit., p. 1961. In summary, the authors write, "This means that national borders mean much less than they used to regarding the flow of technology, at least among the nations that have made the now needed social investments in education and research facilities."

10. As Nathan Rosenberg has written: "The industrialization of the American economy in the nineteenth century focused strongly upon the development of a machine technology. The invention of new machines or machine-made products—cotton gin, reaper, thresher, cultivator, typewriter, barbed wire, revolver, sewing machine, bicycle, and later the automobile—involved the solution of problems which require mechanical skill, ingenuity, and versatility, but not, typically, a recourse to scientific knowledge or elaborate experimental methods" (*Technology and American Economic Growth* [New York: Harper & Row, 1976]), p. 54. Also, see Rosenberg, *Black Box,* on how industrial progress proceeded in small steps, pp. 6–8. On the increasingly scientific nature of industrial technology, see F. Narin and F. Noma, "Is Technology Becoming Science?" *Scienceometrics,* 1985. The authors found that new patent applications made many more references to scientific research than they once did.

11. Until 1989, foreign-owned patents in the United States were rising faster than those granted Americans. Most of this increase was accounted for by Japanese individuals or corporations. The share remained the same in 1990 and was reversed slightly, in favor of American patentors, in 1991, the latest year for which data are available (National Science Board, op. cit., pp. 172–73). For science and engineering bachelor's degrees in the Western countries versus Asia, see ibid., p. xvii.

12. Ibid., p. 100.

13. For example, see Edward A. Gargan, "India Booming as a Leader in Software for Computers," *New York Times,* December 29, 1994.

14. National Science Board, op. cit., pp. 160–61. On developing nations, for example, see Marcus W. Brauchjli, "Indonesia Is Divided Over How to Compete: Low Cost or High Tech," *Wall Street Journal,* April 5, 1993.

15. National Science Board, op. cit., pp. 440–41.

16. Bronwyn H. Hall, "Industrial Research During the 1980s: Did the Rate of Return Fall?" *Brookings Papers: Microeconomics* 2, 1993. It is worthwhile quoting the author at length: "It is hard to escape the conclusion that the differing na-

ture of the competitive challenges in these sectors may have something to do with the apparent differences in the returns to R&D. The electrical and computing sectors have been subject to considerably more entry and competition (much of it of the lower-cost foreign variety) than the chemical and pharmaceutical sectors [who are protected by patents], and this seems to have been reflected in more rapid write-offs of the intangible assets created by R&D investment. In the electrical and particularly computing sectors, product cycles have speeded up, giving less time to reap the returns to R&D, and imitation has in some cases been quite successful and fairly immediate, increasing the private rate of obsolescence."

In fact, so high is the rate of obsolescence in the new computer and telecommunications areas in which so many analysts express confidence that even high levels of capital investment will not affect economic growth overall very much. A recent study shows that this equipment accounts for only about 3.5 percent of all the capital equipment in the nation, so that even if we enjoyed extraordinary rates of return on these ballyhooed investments, they would account for a surprisingly small part of the economy. See Stephen Oliner and Daniel E. Sichel, "Computers and Output Growth Revisited: How Big Is the Puzzle?" *Brookings Papers on Economic Activity*, Winter 1994.

17. In a famous early study ("Research Costs and Social Returns: Hybrid Corn and Related Innovations," *Journal of Political Economy*, October 1958), Zvi Griliches demonstrated that the return to the entire community of the development of hybrid corn came to 40 percent a year. Another example of a public good is Bell Labs' development of the semiconductor (with the later help of government funds). Its return to the community was far greater than its return to Bell Labs. For such reasons, some economists believe we will increasingly need networks of companies to pool resources in order to invest adequately in R&D because the return that would flow to only one company will not be sufficient to compensate for the risk of failure. See Paul Romer, "Implementing a National Technology Strategy with Self-Organizing Industry Investment Boards," *Brookings Papers on Economic Activity*, Vol. 2, 1993.

18. George Gilder, *Recapturing the Spirit of Enterprise* (San Francisco: ICS Press, 1984), especially Chapter 13. John Naisbitt, *Global Paradox: The Bigger the World Economy the More Powerful Its Smallest Player* (New York: William Morrow, 1994).

19. Alvin Toffler and Heidi Toffler, *Creating a New Civilization* (Atlanta: Turner Publishing, 1994). Also, Alvin Toffler, *The Third Wave* (New York: William Morrow, 1980). Piore and Sabel, op. cit., especially Chapter 11. William H. Davidow and Michael S. Malone, *The Virtual Corporation: Structuring and Revitalizing the Corporation for the Twenty-first Century* (New York: HarperCollins, 1992). House Speaker Newt Gingrich professes similar beliefs and is a devotee of the works of the Tofflers, who nevertheless themselves say they are "liber-

als." Gingrich entitled one speech in early 1995 "From Virtuality to Reality." Maureen Dowd, "Capital's Virtual Reality: Gingrich Rides a 3d Wave," *New York Times,* January 11, 1995.

20. Martin Neil Baily and Robert J. Gordon, "The Productivity Slowdown, Measurement Issues, and the Explosion of Computer Power," *Brookings Papers on Economic Activity,* Vol. 2, 1988, p. 361. The authors find, for example, that productivity for "non-goods-producing" industries grew by 2.49 percent a year between 1948 and 1973 and at only .69 percent a year since then. See note 45 of Chapter 2 for other sources.

21. For a typically overenthusiastic article on the prospects for soft production, see Gene Bylinsky, "The Digital Factory," *Fortune,* November 14, 1994.

22. On product cutbacks, Stalk and Webber, op. cit., p. 302. The authors point out how many products have been pruned in recent years by Japanese consumer electronics firms as well as by other consumer products firms. As they summarize, "Companies had to commit more and more human and financial capital at an increasing pace to bring out more and more varieties of products, without any prospect of achieving competitive advantages, higher margins, or more attractive profits." On TV R&D, James Magid, analyst, Needham & Co. (interview with author, February 16, 1995).

23. McKinsey Global Institute, "Productivity in the Computer Industry," pp. 10–11. The authors further write, "The leading and differentiated position of IBM, while limiting the degree of competition during the early stages of the industry, did have numerous positive benefits. The concentrated R&D efforts of IBM led to the development of new technologies and products."

24. Steven E. Prokesch, "Mastering Chaos at the High-Tech Frontier: An Interview with Silicon Graphics's Ed McCracken," *Harvard Business Review,* November–December 1993, p. 140. Jeff Madrick, "Permanent Temps," *NBC Nightly News,* April 10, 1993.

25. Maddison, op. cit., pp. 50–51.

26. A survey by Wyatt Co., for example, found that downsizing and layoffs were usually not "very effective." Gilbert Fuchsberg, "Why Shake-ups Work for Some, Not for Others," *Wall Street Journal,* October 1, 1993. An American Management Association survey found that downsizing improved profits for only 44 percent of companies. "When Lay-offs Alone Don't Turn the Tide," *Business Week,* December 7, 1992. In a review of surveys of firms that adopted a range of manufacturing reforms, from just-in-time inventorying to lean production, team approaches, and total quality management, two Harvard Business School professors say, "While some of these improvement efforts have been successful, the majority, according to recent surveys, have not." Also see Robert H. Hayes

and Gary P. Pisano, "Beyond World Class: The New Manufacturing Strategy," *Harvard Business Review,* January–February 1994.

27. In general, see Chandler, *Scale and Scope.* Also, Bruce Kogut, "National Organizing Principles of Work, and the Erstwhile Dominance of the American Multinational Corporation," in *Industrial and Corporate Change,* 1992.

28. *Multifactor Productivity Measures, 1991 and 1992,* BLS, July 1994.

29. Robert J. Gordon writes that the low return on capital demonstrates that a lack of investment was not our problem in the 1970s and 1980s. "Private investment is ruled out in that the productivity slowdown has occurred not just in labor productivity but also in multi-factor productivity, which takes into account the slower growth of capital input" ("American Economic Growth: One Big Wave?" working paper, Northwestern University, March 1993, footnote on p. 1). While this probably overstates the case, it sheds needed light on the subject. A low return on capital probably resulted from the retreat from mass production and rising competitiveness. But it also resulted from an inability of businessmen to perceive new profitable investment opportunities in an environment that was changing so rapidly.

For an excellent rebuttal of the savings shortfall argument, see Robert A. Blecker, "The New Economic Stagnation," in Bernstein and Adler, eds., op. cit., pp. 278–294.

30. According to the calculations of Robert Lawrence, real interest rates averaged 2.7 percent in the 1960s, when savings were especially high, 1.1 percent in the 1970s, when savings began to falter but inflation soared, and 5.8 percent in the 1980s, when savings rates were low but inflationary expectations remained high as actual inflation subsided. "Time Horizons," pp. 34–35.

31. Among others, Edward Wolff has examined whether capital investment is a cause or a consequence of growing industrial and technological opportunities. He and others conclude that the arrows point both ways. Capital investment both creates opportunities and is a consequence of them. The relative degree to which it is either cause or effect no doubt changes from one period to the next. Wolff, "Capital Formation and Productivity Convergence over the Long Term," *American Economic Review,* June 1991, p. 566. Also, "Capital Formation and Productivity Growth in the 1970s and 1980s: A Comparative Look at OECD Countries," Council on Competitiveness, February 1992.

32. Speaking of the new "middle class" of the mid-nineteenth century, Gordon Wood writes, "The new middle class extolled education, but not a classical or even a liberal arts education. They wanted education that was practical and useful.... Many members of the revolutionary elite, including Benjamin Rush, Noah Webster, and Francis Hopkinson, had even attacked the study of the

'dead languages' of Greek and Latin as time-consuming, useless, and unrepublican. Such study of Greek and Latin, Rush had said, was 'improper in a peculiar manner in the United States' because it confined education only to a few, when in fact republicanism requires everyone to be educated." Wood, op. cit., p. 349, citing Meyer Reinhold, *Classica Americana: The Greek and Roman Heritage in the United States* (Detroit, 1984).

33. Nelson and Wright provide a brief overview of how practically oriented our higher education was, from the agricultural research universities of the nineteenth century to engineering schools in the early twentieth century. Nelson and Wright, op. cit., pp. 1939–40.

34. Richard Freeman, *The Overeducated American* (New York: Academic Press, 1976).

35. Dale W. Jorgenson and Barbara M. Fraumeni, *Investment in Education and U.S. Economic Growth,* from *The U.S. Savings Challenge, Policy Options for Productivity and Growth* (Westview Press, 1990). Also, reprints in Economic Theory and Econometrics, Harvard University.

36. Richard J. Murnane and Frank Levy, "Why Today's High School–Educated Males Earn Less than Their Fathers Did: The Problem and an Assessment of Responses," *Harvard Education Review,* Spring 1993.

37. An excellent summary of research can be found in Frank Levy and Richard J. Murnane, "U.S. Earnings Levels and Earnings Inequality: A Review of Recent Trends and Proposed Explanations," *Journal of Economic Literature,* September 1992. "... the much discussed 'mismatch hypothesis' which holds that the economy is experiencing a growing mismatch between the skills needed in the economy and the skills possessed by the labor force. To date, however, solid evidence on the nature and extent of this mismatch is hard to come by."

38. Mishel and Bernstein, *State of Working America,* p. 138, in 1993 dollars.

39. See again the important paper by Katz and Murphy, op. cit.

40. On the extent that college graduates now take high school jobs, Daniel E. Hecker, "Reconciling Conflicting Data on Jobs for College Graduates," *Monthly Labor Review,* July 1992.

41. See Ashley Dunn, "Skilled Asians Leaving U.S. For High-Tech Jobs at Home," *New York Times,* February 21, 1995.

42. None of this means that a high level of education does not contribute to economic growth. Rather, it is both a cause and a consequence, the degree of which shifts in different periods and under changing circumstances. Economists have generally used statistical methods to determine to what extent the

degree and quality of education is a cause or consequence of growth and opportunity. Most economists would agree that the arrows go both ways, but in recent years I think there has been a strong tendency to overestimate the degree to which education is a cause rather than a consequence, especially in times of slow economic growth. It might be more useful to see education as a necessary but not sufficient condition for growth. For a succinct representative discussion of this issue, see Baumol, Blackman, and Wolff, op. cit., pp. 200–206.

43. For example, see "World Report," *U.S. News and World Report,* November 22, 1993, p. 35.

44. For a general discussion, see Laura D'Andrea Tyson, William Dickens, and John Zysman, eds., *The Dynamics of Trade and Employment* (Cambridge: Ballinger Publishing Co., 1988). Paul R. Krugman, ed., *Strategic Trade Policy and the New International Economics* (Cambridge: MIT Press, 1986).

45. *Equity Capital Outflows,* BEA, Department of Commerce. These represent equity investments by American corporations or investors of a minimum of 10 percent or more in a foreign company or venture.

46. Sachs and Shatz, op. cit., p. 39.

47. On the anxiety of early Americans, see in general Lewis O. Saum, *The Popular Mood of Pre–Civil War America* (Westport, Conn.: Greenwood Press, 1980). On the Second Great Awakening, see especially Nathan O. Hatch, *Democratization of American Christianity* (New Haven: Yale University Press, 1989). "However diverse these theologies," writes Hatch, "they all offered common people, especially the poor, compelling visions of individual self-respect and collective self-confidence." I am especially indebted to Sean Wilentz for his comments on these issues.

William James summarized what he called the evangelical "mind cure" this way in *The Varieties of Religious Experience:* "Give up the feeling of responsibility, let go your hold, resign the care of your destiny to higher powers, be genuinely indifferent as to what becomes of it all, and you will find that you gain a perfect inward relief, but often also, in addition, the particular goods you sincerely thought you were renouncing," cited by Gary Wills, *Reagan's America* (New York: Penguin, 1985), p. 456.

48. As Charles Sellers writes, "Like the New Divinity and the new women's consciousness, every popular cultural or political movement in the early republic arose originally against the market. Yet under the daily pressure of competitive imperatives on participants' lives, every such movement eventually became a mode of accommodating to capitalist necessity." Op. cit., p. 208.

49. Hofstadter, op. cit., p. 412.

50. Gary Wills, op. cit., p. 456.

51. Douglas Jekhl, "Clinton Urges Young to Reject Pessimism," *New York Times,* May 20, 1994.

52. Mickey Kaus, *The End of Equality* (New York: Basic Books, 1992) p. 5.

53. Richard L. Berke, "Survey Finds Voters in U.S. Rootless and Self-absorbed," *New York Times,* September 15, 1994.

54. Ralph Waldo Emerson, "Self-Reliance," in *The Selected Writings of Ralph Waldo Emerson* (New York: Modern Library, 1992).

55. William James, "Pragmatism and Religion," in *Pragmatism* (Cambridge: Harvard University Press, a Harvard Paperback, 1975), p. 137.

CHAPTER 5. LOST BEARINGS

1. On the seeming surprise among legislators when the Congressional Budget Office computed how much the Clinton health plan would really cost, see Adam Clymer, "Full of Sound and Fury, Signifying . . . Well, Something," *New York Times,* August 21, 1994. Also Herbert Stein, "The Tangled Web of Health Care Reform," *Wall Street Journal,* August 18, 1994. Also see two reports by William Dudley, *The Administration's Healthcare Plan: Too Good to Be True?* (October 1993), and *The Clinton Healthcare Plan: No Free Lunch* (January 1994), U.S. Economic Research, Goldman Sachs & Co. New York. On the political gridlock that resulted, see Robin Toner, "The Art of Reprocessing the Democratic Process," *New York Times,* September 4, 1994.

2. Theda Skocpol, *Protecting Soldiers and Mothers: The Political Origins of Social Policy in the United States* (Cambridge: Belknap Press, 1992). The outlay came to as much as two thirds of federal receipts in these years. See pp. 110–14.

3. For a discussion of the rising after-tax income in the 1960s, see Levy, *Dollars and Cents,* pp. 55–60. The tax burden of the typical family rose from 13.1 percent of family income in 1959 to 20.9 percent in 1969, but incomes grew so quickly, we were willing to bear the burden.

4. A survey of everyday material life in America, from which these facts are drawn, can be found in Lance E. Davis et al., *American Economic Growth: An Economist's History of the United States* (New York: Harper & Row, 1972), pp. 61–89.

5. Ibid., p. 67. "The sewing machine . . . affected the manner of living more than any other labor-saving device." Improvements in sewing machines also enabled factories to produce shoes and clothing. Chandler, *Visible Hand,* p. 246. By 1860 about 275,000 sewing machines were being sold a year.

6. We reached "universal" education at the primary level well before Britain or France did. Richard A. Easterlin, "Why Isn't the Whole World Developed?" *Journal of Economic History,* March 1981.

7. Irvin G. Wylie, *The Self-Made Man in America* (New York: Free Press, 1954). Wylie writes, "At mid-century the young man who went to church, or to the lyceum, or to the reading rooms of a mercantile library association was bound to hear or read something about the self-made man and his glorious conquest of fortune," p. 9.

8. Stanley Lebergott, op. cit. On autos, p. 130; on appliances, pp. 112–13. Levy, *Dollars and Dreams,* on autos and houses, p. 50.

9. Philip Seib, *Rush Hour* (Fort Worth, Tex.: The Summit Group, 1994), p. 157.

10. Claudia Goldin, "How America Graduated from High School: 1910 to 1960," National Bureau of Economic Research, working paper No. 4762, especially p. 15.

11. Wood, op. cit., p. 347. The term "middling" was becoming more commonly used. There were, of course, poor people and slaves, and the inequality of incomes grew since colonial years. But this must be viewed, as Wood says, in the context of the world Americans came from. Wood writes: "We today see the distinctions of early-nineteenth-century society vividly, not only those between free and enslaved, white and black, male and female, but those between rich and poor, educated and barely literate. Yet if we are to understand the wonder, the astonishment, and judgments of [contemporary] observers . . . , we must see, as they did, this society of the early Republic in the context of what American society had once been and what societies elsewhere in the Western world still resembled. In that context America had experienced an unprecedented democratic revolution and had created a huge sprawling society that was more egalitarian, more middling, and more dominated by the interests of ordinary people than any that had ever existed before," p. 348.

12. Levy, *Dollars and Dreams,* pp. 24–25. Lebergott, op. cit., pp. 111–13, 130.

13. Levy, *Dollars and Dreams,* p. 59.

14. Mishel and Bernstein, *State of Working America,* p. 26.

15. Lebergott, op. cit., pp. 103–13, 130. Levy, *Dollars and Dreams,* p. 25.

16. *Historical Statistics of the United States, Colonial Times to 1970,* Bureau of the Census, *Statistical Abstracts of the United States,* 1994.

17. Paul Yakoboski and Celia Silverman, *Retirement Income Security: The Situation of Current Retirees and Prospects for Current Workers,* Washington, D.C., Employee Benefit Research Institute, May 1994, Executive Summary, p. 3.

18. It is certainly clear that relatively few made it all the way from rags to riches. See Edward Pessen, ed., *Three Centuries of Social Mobility in America* (Lexington, Mass.: D.C. Heath & Co., 1974). But a more modest but widespread degree of social mobility has been persuasively documented by scholars. Probably the best example is included in the Pessen book. Stephan Thernstrom, "Working-Class Upward Mobility in Newburyport," pp. 144–164. "By 1880, the undifferentiated mass of poverty-stricken laboring families [from 1850]," writes Thernstrom, "had separated into three layers. On top was a small but significant elite of laboring families who had gained a foothold in the low fringes of the middle-class occupational world. Below them was the large body of families who had attained property mobility while remaining in manual occupations, most often of the unskilled or semiskilled variety; these families constituted the stable, respectable, home-owning stratum of the Newburyport working class. At the very bottom of the social ladder was the impoverished, floating lower class, large in number but so transient as to be formless and powerless.... The contradiction between an ideology of limitless opportunity and the realities of working-class existence is unlikely to have dismayed men whose aspirations and expectations were shaped in the Irish village or the New England subsistence farm. The 'dream of success' certainly affected these laboring families, but the personal measure of success was modest. By this measure, the great majority of them had indeed 'gotten ahead,' " pp. 159, 164. Also see Thernstrom, *The Other Bostonians* (Cambridge: Harvard University Press, 1973).

As Gordon Wood writes of an earlier period, it increasingly became self-interest that held the nation together as incomes rose and opportunity spread. "Many Federalists and Republicans, like many Whigs and Democrats later, concluded that interest was about all most Americans had in common. They could not be controlled by force, or else they would have no liberty. But appeals to virtue could not contain these people either. Only interest could restrain them. Americans govern themselves, they said, because it was in their interest to do so. The desire to make money and get ahead helped them to develop habits of self-control." Wood, op. cit., p. 336.

19. In general, see Margo, "Labor in the Nineteenth Century," pp. 11–15. For a more detailed analysis of pre–Civil War wages, see Robert A. Margo and Georgia Villaflor, "The Growth of Wages in Antebellum America: New Evidence," *Journal of Economic History,* December 1987. The authors find that, contrary to the pessimists' claim that the wages did not rise, they did in fact rise significantly. However, contrary to the optimists' belief, they rose erratically. Sharp if temporary downturns in average real wages help explain the strong rise of labor unions and other reform groups as early as the 1830s. For cyclical variability of wage increases, which was significant if of short duration in the nineteenth century, see Margo, "Labor in the Nineteenth Century," pp. 20–22. For the second half of the nineteenth and all of the twentieth century, average real

wages can be found in *Historical Statistics* and the *U.S. Statistical Abstracts,* Bureau of the Census, Washington, D.C.

On unemployment, see Margo, "Labor in the Nineteenth Century," pp. 39–42. Goldin, "Labor in the Twentieth Century," pp. 26–34. Goldin summarizes the recent work of Christina Romer on the reduced severity of the business cycle in the nineteenth century, and the resulting reduction in estimates of the unemployment rate. Also see Margo and Goldin, "Downtime: Voluntary and Involuntary Unemployment of the Past and Present," National Bureau of Economic Research.

20. Ibid., p. 15. Margo estimates average real wages were 270 percent to 330 percent higher in 1900 than in 1800. On the twentieth century, see Lebergott, op. cit., p. 76.

21. On the display of materialism, see Wood, op. cit., p. 233. Sedgwick quoted by Wood, p. 342.

22. Even had the wage of the typical worker merely stagnated or been up slightly over these years, it would have been the worst twenty-year performance since the early 1800s with the exception of the Civil War aftermath.

23. Mishel and Bernstein, *State of Working America*, p. 32.

24. A Gallup Organization survey, "Confidence Gap: Press Trapped in Own Cynicism," *Wall Street Journal,* August 31, 1994. On the wrong direction, NBC News/*Wall Street Journal* poll, "America's New Crusade," *U.S. News & World Report,* August 1, 1994, p. 27.

25. Times Mirror Center poll, Richard L. Berke, "From Not Quite Acceptable to Maybe Even Electable," *New York Times,* October 2, 1994.

26. Karen DeWitt, "Cold Shoulder to Churches That Practice Preachings," *New York Times,* March 27, 1994.

27. Associated Press, "School District Ousts Principal in Alabama," *New York Times,* August 8, 1994.

28. Diana Jean Schemo, "Persistent Racial Segregation Mars Suburbs' Green Dream," *New York Times,* March 17, 1994.

29. Larry Rohter, "Battle over Patriotism Curriculum," *New York Times,* May 15, 1994.

30. Levy et al., op. cit. Also, Levy, *Dollars and Dreams,* pp. 79–81.

31. Murnane and Levy, "Earnings Levels," p. 1361. Murnane and Levy, "Why Today's," p. 2. High school dropouts did far worse, their average earnings down by 36 percent.

32. John Bound and Richard B. Freeman, "What Went Wrong? The Erosion of Relative Earnings and Employment Among Young Black Men in the 1980s," *Quarterly Journal of Economics,* February 1992.

33. Commission on Worker-Management Relations, op. cit., pp. 15–16. *Economic Report of the President,* 1994, Council of Economic Advisers, Washington, D.C., pp. 105–13. Also see "Gross Job Flows in Manufacturing," Center for Economic Studies, Federal Reserve System, 1994. Mishel and Bernstein, *State of Working America,* pp. 205–14.

34. Murnane and Levy, "Education and Skills for the U.S. Work Force," pp. 50–52. Louis Uchitelle, "Middle-Aged, Male, Educated and Falling Behind," *New York Times,* February 10, 1994.

35. Commission on Worker-Management Relations, op. cit., p. 16.

36. Dun & Bradstreet Corp., *Total Business Failures,* New York, September 1994.

37. Bureau of the Census, "Income, Poverty, and Valuation of Noncash Benefits, 1993," Department of Commerce. Updated by Bureau of the Census, "Income, Poverty and Health Insurance," October 1994 (Commission on Worker-Management Relations, op. cit., p. 18).

38. Income and poverty estimates, Bureau of the Census, press briefing by Daniel H. Weinberg, chief of Housing and Household Economic Statistics Division. Also, author analysis of Bureau of Census data and the family income data in Mishel and Bernstein, *State of Working America,* p. 34. As Mishel and Bernstein point out, the top 20 percent of the population earned its highest share of income in the postwar period. Also see *Economic Report of the President,* 1994, p. 117.

39. Commission on Worker-Management Relations, op. cit., p. 19.

40. BLS data on manufacturing workweek. "The Great American Time Squeeze," Laura Leete-Guy and Juliet B. Schor, Economic Policy Institute, Washington, D.C., 1993. These data are based on those who work full-time. In 1993 manufacturing hours worked hit a post-1945 high. Amanda Bennet, "In Factories, a New Day Dawns—a Longer One," *Wall Street Journal,* January 17, 1994. Surveys of work time that include the total population do not take account of the rapidly growing number of involuntary part-time workers, involuntary early retirees, and a high number of discouraged workers who have dropped out of the workforce altogether. Such surveys understate the hours worked. There are now 1.1 million discouraged workers in America, up by about 60 percent from ten years ago, for example. On involuntary free time, see Sylvia Nassar, "More Men in Prime of Life Spend Less Time Working," *New York Times,* December 1, 1994.

41. Louis Uchitelle, "Moonlighting Plus: 3-Job Families on the Rise," *New York Times,* August 16, 1994.

42. Mishel and Bernstein, *State of Working America,* pp. 37–42.

43. Joint Center for Housing Studies, op. cit., p. 10.

44. Mortgage Bankers Association, *Percent of Loans in Foreclosure,* Washington, D.C., 1994

45. Author analysis of data of American Automobile Association, *Total Vehicle Sales and Vehicles in Use.* In 1973 more than 18 vehicles per hundred workers were purchased compared to less than 12 vehicles per hundred in 1993. Per capita, there were about 8 cars per hundred Americans bought in 1973 compared to about 6 per hundred in 1993.

Durability cannot account for these shifts. The age of cars in operation began to rise in the 1970s and 1980s, which is what enabled the number of cars per household to remain about the same. These American cars, manufactured in the 1960s, 1970s, and early 1980s, were not appreciably more durable than their predecessors. American cars were made more durable beginning in the latter half of the 1980s. The one third of cars in 1992 that were ten years or older for the most part were manufactured in the late 1970s and early 1980s. For a characteristic article that misstates the causes of reduced auto purchases, see Oscar Suris and Garriela Stern, "Six Reasons People Are Buying Few New Cars," *Wall Street Journal,* May 6, 1995. Among the reasons other than durability that account for reduced sales, the authors say, personal computers and kitchens are simply more popular than cars these days. Computers are, of course, also a lot less expensive than cars, just as fixing up your kitchen is a lot less expensive than buying a new house. Fashion is dictated by what people can afford. Only a few days before this article appeared the Commerce Department reported that the average wages and benefits of all workers (Employment Cost Index) had not risen at all in the twelve months ending March 1995 after inflation, despite the economic expansion. The authors did not mention this at all. I do not blame them in particular. They are merely reflecting the prevailing misunderstanding of the influences of slow economic growth.

46. Douglas Lavin, "Stiff Showroom Prices Drive More Americans to Purchase Used Cars," *Wall Street Journal,* November 1, 1994.

47. Mishel and Bernstein, *State of Working America,* pp. 247–53. Associated Press, "Price of Higher Education Becomes Even Dearer," *New York Times,* September 27, 1994. G. Pascal Zachary, "Parents' Gifts to Adult Children Studied," *Wall Street Journal,* February 9, 1995. *The Economist,* "Running to Stand Still," November 10, 1990.

48. Peter Passell, "After Years of Trying to Fix Education, Why Isn't It Fixed?"

New York Times, October 13, 1994. Raymond Hernandez, "Revolt Against School Spending Reaches the Wealthiest Suburbs," *New York Times,* January 18, 1995.

49. David E. Bloom and Richard B. Freeman, "The Falling Private Pension Coverage in the U.S.," Working Paper No. 3973, National Bureau of Economic Research, Cambridge, Mass., 1992 Participation rates have probably risen slightly in the past few years, but this should be treated cautiously. As we noted in the text, pension plans are becoming more stringent. An increasing number require employee contributions, for example. Most new ones are defined contribution rather than defined benefit plans, as noted. Nor do we know yet whether employee tenures in corporations will begin to decline dramatically, which would mean that benefits earned will be reduced as workers leave jobs early. As yet, tenure rates have not fallen dramatically in the aggregate, but if slow growth continues, they may well do so.

50. Congressional Budget Office, *Baby Boomers in Retirement: An Early Perspective,* Washington, D.C., September 1993.

51. A study by Arthur D. Little and WEFA, two consulting firms, cited in B. Douglas Bernheim, *The Adequacy of Saving for Retirement: Are the Baby Boomers on Track?* For the Employee Benefit Research Institute, Washington, D.C., May 1994.

52. Employee Benefit Research Institute, Washington, D.C.

53. Alan J. Auerbach and Laurence J. Kotlikoff, *The United States' Fiscal and Savings Crises and Their Implications for the Baby Boom Generation,* Employee Benefit Research Institute, Washington, D.C., May 1994, pp. 5, 7. A tax increase of 5 percent rests on fairly pessimistic assumptions about the population growth into the mid-twenty-first century. A more intermediate tax hike of 1.5 to 3 percentage points, however, is a highly reasonable possibility if the rate of productivity growth remains slow.

54. A random example is Tim W. Ferguson, "Days of Whine and Poses," *Wall Street Journal,* March 1, 1994.

55. Edward Denison, a pioneering economist in the study of productivity, warned against such comparative analyses as early as 1971. See Edward F. Denison, "Welfare Measurement and the GNP," *Survey of Current Business,* January 1971.

56. "A Tale of Two Suburbias," *U.S. News & World Report,* a survey of six representative metropolitan areas, November 9, 1992. In general, the population is leaving older suburbs for the outlying suburbs and rural areas. The prospect is that these older suburbs may now be left to decline as the inner cities have been.

CHAPTER 6. WHAT WE FACE

1. See Chapter 1.

2. BLS computation done for the author over the course of the business cycle to date. As of December 1994, after fifteen quarters, the annual rate of productivity growth was 2.2 percent in the latest business recovery and expansion compared with 2.0 percent in the 1970s over a comparable period of the business cycle, and 1.9 percent in the 1980s. As of this writing, the cycle is not complete, so any historical comparisons would be premature.

Some economists claim productivity growth would have been faster in the 1990s had output grown as rapidly as it had in the 1970s and 1980s. At the very least, this begs the question, however. Growth was moderate partly because our ability to produce was constrained by slow productivity growth. Moreover, the most rapid gains in productivity generally come over the initial output gains.

Some economists also point out that the 1991 low in productivity was a "high" low because the last recession was moderate. They prefer to measure productivity growth from the last peak, which would show slightly faster productivity growth than in the seventies and eighties to this point, if only very slightly faster. The problem with this calculation is that the last peak was a "low" one by historical standards, the rate of growth very slow in the year or two before the recession began. See *Economic Report of the President*, 1995, Chapter 2, for the most serious optimistic analysis of recent productivity growth. The Council of Economic Advisers finds an improvement of only a couple of tenths of a percent. What's more, even this marginal improvement will be revised away when new price data take into account the sharp reduction in computer prices. Computation by Dan Sichel, Brookings Institution, for the author, March 1995.

In sum, however productivity growth is measured as of this writing, there is no evidence of a rebound. As yet, any such claims are a leap of faith. By comparison it should be noted that annualized productivity growth as of fifteen quarters into the business cycles of the 1950s and 1960s came to 4.8 percent and 4.1 percent, respectively, twice as fast as recent rates of growth.

3. BLS, Office of Compensation and Working Conditions.

4. For example, the Federal Reserve reported that consumer installment debt rose at an annual rate of 17.3 percent in November 1994.

5. *Economic Report of the President*, 1994, p. 82.

6. Charles A. Murray, *Losing Ground: American Social Policy, 1950–80* (New York: Basic Books, 1984).

7. Bureau of the Census, "Income, Poverty, and Health Insurance." Adjustments to the poverty rate that take into account noncash benefits, taxes, and different

measurements of inflation reduce the absolute level of poverty. But they do not in any way change the direction of the incidence of poverty, which rose inexorably throughout the 1980s. Income and poverty estimates given by Daniel H. Weinberg in a press briefing.

8. As the Census Bureau has reported, 18 percent of full-time workers are officially poor. These include many young workers, but the rate of increase has been extraordinary. See Chapter 5.

9. National Science Board, op. cit., 1993, p. 91.

10. Olinor and Sichel, op. cit.

11. Alan B. Krueger, "How Computers Have Changed the Wage Structure," *Quarterly Journal of Economics,* February 1993.

12. The value of our minimum wage, for example, has fallen by 31 percent after inflation since 1979 (measured in 1993 dollars). In times of slow economic growth, the low minimum wage has probably contributed to declining wages. Many economists argue a higher minimum wage would retard the growth in the number of jobs. This has been challenged by David Card and Alan B. Krueger, *Myth and Measurement: The New Economics of the Minimum Wage* (Princeton: Princeton University Press, 1995).

13. Commission on Worker-Management Relations, op. cit., p. 19. Data on workplace accidents from National Safety Workplace Institute, Chicago.

14. On job training, see especially Thomas A. Kochan and Paul Osterman, "Human Resources Development and Utilization," MIT, Council on Competitiveness, February 1991.

15. In World War I and World War II, the distribution of income narrowed sharply, which may have made higher taxes more palatable to most Americans, but at the least reduced some of the burden. Lee and Passell, op. cit., pp. 338–41. Robert Margo and Claudia Goldin, "The Great Compression," *Quarterly Journal of Economics,* February 1992. The early history of American taxes was more a matter of punishing one region of the country to benefit most of the rest of the country—typically by favoring manufacturers by imposing high tariffs on imports at the expense of our agricultural exporters.

16. The United Steelworkers Union president Lynn Williams, for example, could not get his members to reduce overtime voluntarily in order to share jobs with more workers. Jeff Madrick, "Should Americans Have Shorter Work Weeks," *NBC Nightly News,* July 31, 1993. By contrast, Europeans are more open (if not universally) to the idea and put it into practice. Roger Cohen, "Europeans Ponder Working Less So More of Them Can Have Jobs," *New York Times,* November 22, 1993. Europeans have also been generally willing to raise taxes

broadly during the 1990s recession. Nathaniel C. Nash, "Europeans Shrug as Taxes Go Up," *New York Times*, February 16, 1995.

17. For an analysis of how Reagan economists oversold what they had accomplished, see Benjamin Friedman, *Day of Reckoning: The Consequences of American Economic Policy Under Reagan and After* (New York: Random House, 1988), pp. 187–208.

On income distribution, between 1977 and 1989, 60 percent of pretax income was earned by the top 1 percent of families. Their share of income rose from 9 percent of income to 13 percent. Sylvia Nasar, "The 1980s: A Very Good Time for the Very Rich," *New York Times,* March 5, 1992. This computation includes capital gains and interest income.

18. *Wall Street Journal*/NBC News poll. Gerald F. Seib and Joe Davidson, "Whites, Blacks Agree on Problems; The Issue Is How to Solve Them," *Wall Street Journal,* September 29, 1994. Former Education Secretary William Bennett's book on moral choices, *The Book of Virtues* (New York: Simon & Schuster, 1994), sold more than 1.5 million copies as of the fall of 1994. Magazines were full of commentaries calling for moral regeneration. For example, see two op-ed pieces published in *The Wall Street Journal* within days of each other: Don Eberly, "Even Newt Can't Save Us," February 3, 1995, and Gertrude Himmelfarb, "Re-Moralizing America," February 7, 1995.

19. Commission on Worker-Management Relations, op. cit., p. 22.

20. I include food stamps and traditional aid to dependent mothers in the total welfare budget.

21. Maddison, op. cit., p. 53. See also Edward N. Wolff, "Capital Formation and Productivity Growth in the 1970s and 1980s: A Comparative Look at OECD Countries," New York University, February 1992.

22. *New York Times*/CBS News Poll. Katharine Q. Seelye, "Voters Disgusted With Politicians as Election Nears," *New York Times,* November 3, 1994. Health was the second most important issue in a September poll and had since dropped to fifth place tied with drugs.

23. Goldin, "Labor Markets in the Twentieth Century," p. 10.

24. On how the frontier reduced patriarchal control, see Gerald R. Leslie, *The Family in Social Context* (Oxford: Oxford University Press, 1967). On the damage done to families by industrialization in the nineteenth century, Eli Zaretsky, *Capitalism, The Family and Personal Life* (New York: Harper Colophon Books, 1973). On how the nuclear family was more a creation of the 1950s than a fact of American history, see Stephen Coontz, *The Way We Never Were: American Families and the Nostalgia Trap* (New York: Basic Books, 1993).

25. Near his death, Jefferson was upset with everything from paper money to the rise of evangelical Christianity as well as the growing popularity of a ruffian named Andrew Jackson. Wood., op. cit., p. 367.

26. Walt Whitman, "Notes For Lectures on Democracy and 'Adhesiveness,' " in Clifton J. Furness, *Walt Whitman's Workshop* (New York: Russell & Russell, 1964). Whitman, of course, remained determinedly optimistic. "I will not gloss over the appalling dangers of universal suffrage in the United States. In fact, it is to admit and face these dangers I am writing," he wrote. "The United States are destined either to surmount the gorgeous history of feudalism, or else prove the most tremendous failure of all time. Not the least doubtful am I on any prospects of their material success." But Whitman did not believe that economic growth was enough: "I say that democracy can never prove itself beyond cavil, until it founds and luxuriantly grows its own forms of art, poems, schools, theology, displacing all that exists, or that has been produced anywhere in the past" ("Democratic Vistas," *Complete Prose Works,* 1892, pp. 363–64). In terms of the stability of the nation, we obviously muddled through, anyway. Whether or not we have succeeded on other grounds, grounds that some may argue are more central, is another matter.

27. On changing expectations over time in England, for example, B. Seebohm Rowntree found that by 1899 standards no one in the city of York would have been considered poor at the mid-twentieth century. See Rowntree and G. R. Lavers, *Poverty and the Welfare State: A Third Social Survey of York Dealing Only with Economic Questions* (London: Green & Co., 1951). Cited by Oscar Ornati, *Poverty Amid Affluence,* The Twentieth Century Fund, New York, 1966, pp. 32–33.

APPENDIX

Figure 1 / A SHARP SLOWDOWN

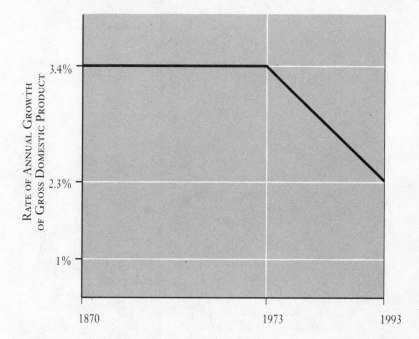

Figure 2 / THOUGH WE GREW RAPIDLY IN SOME YEARS,
GROWTH SINCE 1973 HAS REMAINED SLOW

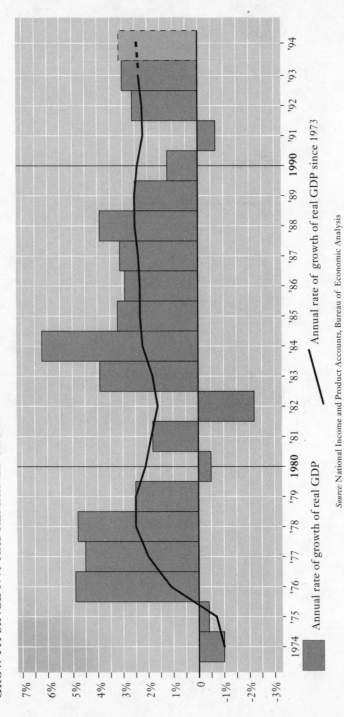

Source: National Income and Product Accounts, Bureau of Economic Analysis

Annual rate of growth of real GDP

Annual rate of growth of real GDP since 1973

Figure 3 / U.S. PRODUCTIVITY GROWTH

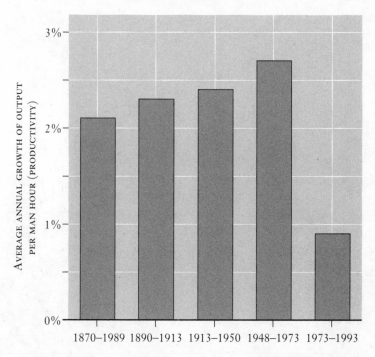

Source: Angus Maddison, *Dynamic Forces in Capitalist Development*

Figure 4 / THE AVERAGE WAGE FALLS

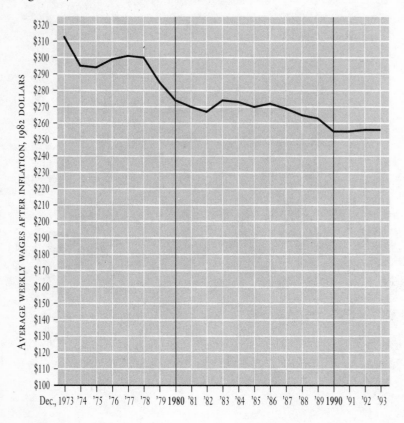

Figure 5 / THE U.S. PRODUCTIVITY LEAD, 1913

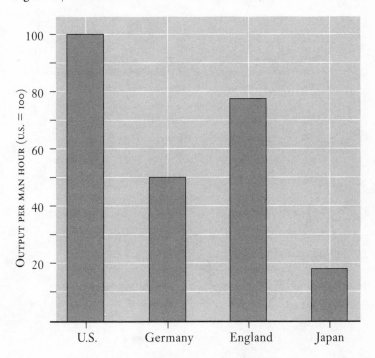

Source: Angus Maddison, Dynamic Forces in Capitalist Development

Figure 6 / WHAT WE LOST

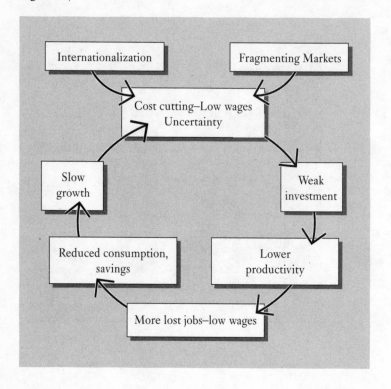

Figure 7 / HOME OWNERSHIP FALLS SHARPLY
IN PRIME BUYING AGE GROUPS

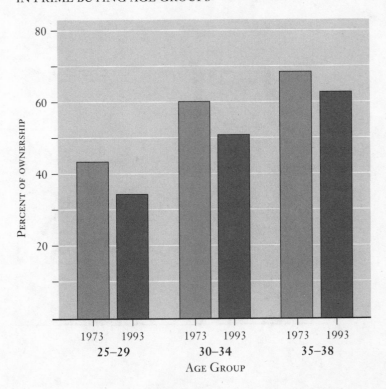

Source: Joint Center for Housing Studies of Harvard University

Figure 8 / WORKERS BUY FEWER CARS AND TRUCKS

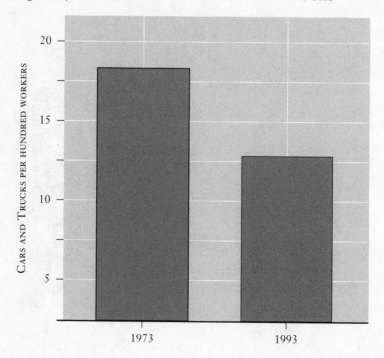

INDEX

Page numbers in *italics* refer to figures.

Thailand, 71
threshers, 143
Timex, 34
tobacco industry, 46–47, 50, 123
Toffler, Alvin, 101, 186*n*–87*n*
tools, 29, 70, 71, 76, 80, 98
toys, 70, 71
trade:
    foreign, 28, 29, 38, 48, 65, 66–67,
        68, 70–72, 113
    free, 65–66, 112
    international, 65, 67, 178*n*–79*n*
"Trade, Jobs, and Wages" (Krugman
        and Lawrence), 178*n*
transistors, 34
transportation, 10, 11, 29–30, 41,
        42–45, 61, 143, 144, 160, 162
Turner, Frederick Jackson, 22–27,
        30–31, 35, 96, 119, 127, 171*n*
turnpikes, 42

unemployment:
    duration of, 88–89, 127
    industrialization and, 31–32
    layoffs and, 88–89, 118–19, 137
    Protestant ethic and, 26
    rate of, 20, 34, 90, 127, 136, 137,
        163
unemployment insurance, 21, 122
unions, labor, 32, 62, 82, 118, 132,
        154, 155, 170*n*–71*n*
United States:
    agrarianism in, 22–27, 30, 32, 38,
        123, 131–32, 143
    economy of, *see* economy, U.S.
    foreign trade of, 28, 29, 38, 48, 65,
        66–67, 68, 70–72, 113
    frontier of, 22–27, 30–31, 35, 38,
        91, 158
    ideology of, 25–27, 31, 32, 35,
        155–58, 162–64
    imports by, 66, 70–72

industrialization of, 13, 22, 23–24,
        27–33, 39, 43, 131–32, 143, 185*n*
land ownership in, 22–28, 29, 124,
        161–62
living standards in, 13–14, 17, 25,
        32, 36, 54, 70, 90, 110, 122–29,
        139, 144–45, 151, 162–63
opportunity in, 23, 31, 133, 158
scientific revolution in, 95–96, 98,
        100
territorial expansion of, 22–24
trade deficit of, 68, 70, 71–72, 113
urbanization of, 24–25, 31, 32, 45,
        132
unwed mothers, 131, 158
urbanization, 24–25, 31, 32, 45, 132

VCRs, 143
video games, 76
Vietnam war, 19, 122
Virtual Corporation, The (Davidow and
        Malone), 102
voting rights, 132

wages and salaries, *see* income
Wall Street Journal, 149
washing machines, 56, 124, 125
wealth, 125–26, 127, 132
welfare, 3, 151, 152, 156, 157, 160,
        163
Westinghouse, 57, 61
wheat, 28, 45
Whitman, Walt, 161, 201*n*
Whitney, Eli, 39
wholesale, 49, 59, 89
women's movement, 116, 129,
        132–33
Wood, Gordon, 188*n*–89*n*
Woolworth, 50
workers:
    benefits of, 16, 62, 88, 122, 141–42,
        154, 167*n*, 197*n*

ABOUT THE AUTHOR

A graduate of Harvard Business School, JEFFREY MADRICK was an Emmy Award–winning economics reporter for NBC from 1985 to 1993. He was finance editor of *Business Week* and a columnist for *Money*, and has written articles on the American economy for many other publications, including *The New York Times, New York Newsday, Global Finance, Institutional Investor*, and *The New York Review of Books*. He lives in New York City.

ABOUT THE TYPE

The text of this book was set in Janson, a misnamed typeface designed in about 1690 by Nicholas Kis, a Hungarian in Amsterdam. In 1919 the matrices became the property of the Stempel Foundry in Frankfurt. It is an old-style book face of excellent clarity and sharpness. Janson serifs are concave and splayed; the contrast between thick and thin strokes is marked.